TOWER HAMLETS COLLEGE
Learning Centre

NOTES ✔ KT-450-445

Editors: Professor A.N. Jeffares (*University* *of Stirling*) & Professor Suheil Bushrui (*American University of Beirut*)

Oscar Wilde

THE IMPORTANCE OF BEING EARNEST

Notes by Christopher S. Nassaar

BA (BEIRUT) MA (SUSSEX) PH D (WISCONSIN)
Assistant Professor, American University of Beirut

LONGMAN
YORK PRESS

YORK PRESS
Immeuble Esseily, Place Riad Solh, Beirut.

ADDISON WESLEY LONGMAN LIMITED
Edinburgh Gate, Harlow,
Essex CM20 2JE, England
Associated companies, branches and representatives
throughout the world

© Librairie du Liban 1980

All rights reserved; no part of this publication may be reproduced,
stored in a retrieval system, or transmitted in any form or by any
means, electronic, mechanical, photocopying, recording, or otherwise
without either the prior written permission of the Publishers or a
licence permitting restricted copying in the United Kingdom issued by
the Copyright Licensing Agency Ltd, 90 Tottenham Court Road, London W1P 9HE.

First published 1980
Sixteenth impression 1998

ISBN 0-582-02272-X

Printed in Singapore through Addison Wesley Longman China Limited

822·8 WIL

058690

Contents

Part 1

Introduction

The life of Oscar Wilde

Oscar Wilde (1854–1900) first attracted public attention as a sort of clown with a great conversational talent. He preached that the pursuit of beauty is the most crucial thing in life, and he went about teaching people how to dress and how to decorate their homes. He himself dressed in a very flashy way that made him the subject of many jokes. Then he went on to write some fairy tales and a novel, *The Picture of Dorian Gray*. The novel, which deals with the evil in human nature and the pursuit of evil beauty, was condemned as immoral by many people, but it was widely read and it helped to establish Wilde as a literary figure. Real success came, however, with a series of plays that dominated the London stage – *Lady Windermere's Fan, A Woman of No Importance, An Ideal Husband,* and finally *The Importance of Being Earnest.* People were amused and entertained by those plays, and Wilde's reputation soared. Especially attractive were the brilliant witty statements that filled the plays. At the height of his success, though, tragedy struck. He was convicted of homosexual practices and sentenced to two years in prison with hard labour. His prison experiences broke his spirit and destroyed his health. On his release, he found himself a rejected man in England, and so went to France, where he was to spend the last few years of his life. He died in poverty in a third-class hotel in Paris.

Early life and Oxford

Wilde was born in Dublin, Ireland, in 1854. His parents were distinguished but highly eccentric. The father, Sir William Wilde, was a well-known and successful Dublin doctor, but he was famous in Dublin not only for the practice of medicine but also for his personal untidiness and uncleanliness. He paid no attention to clothes and rarely ever bathed. Thus, there was usually a thin layer of dirt on his skin, and his fingernails were black. He was also famous for his many love affairs. Despite his unattractive appearance – or perhaps because of it – he insisted on conquering the hearts of as many ladies as possible. One of his love affairs ended in a lawsuit and created a great scandal. While

Sir William was a very short man, almost a dwarf, Wilde's mother was an unusually tall and well-built woman, so that the two together must have presented a comic appearance. In her own way, Lady Wilde was as eccentric as her husband. A good-looking woman, her main concern in youth was politics, and she became an Irish revolutionary seeking to liberate Ireland from British rule. Under the name 'Speranza', she published a volume of mainly revolutionary poems. She drifted away from politics in later years, but remained eccentric if also clever and well-read.

Oscar Fingal O'Flaherty Wills Wilde (this was his full name) spent the first ten years of his life at home, where he was tutored privately. At ten, he was sent to Portora Royal School, one of the best schools in Ireland, where he remained for seven years. He then went to Trinity College, Dublin, for three years, where he was influenced by John Pentland Mahaffy, a famous classical scholar. At the age of twenty he won a scholarship that allowed him to go to Magdalen College, Oxford. As a schoolboy he began to develop and perfect the wit for which he was to become famous. His witty conversation won him the admiration of many of his schoolmates. At Oxford he made full use of his wit to gain attention, and also began to dress in a very dandiacal, flashy manner. In his pursuit of beauty he also decorated his rooms, filling them with a collection of porcelain. Some of his college mates, masculine and athletic, found his ways effeminate and decided to smash up his rooms. Wilde, however, took after his mother physically. Very tall and large-boned, he was able to repel the attack, tossing one of the assailants down the stairs. Having proved his masculinity, he then invited the attackers to his rooms for a drink.

Two men greatly influenced Wilde's development and helped to shape his intellect at Oxford – John Ruskin and Walter Pater. Ruskin, who was Slade Professor of Art, was a deeply religious man who insisted that literature and painting should ally themselves with morality, and who preached the dignity of labour. One of his projects was to organise Oxford undergraduates to build a road between two villages, and thus instruct those upper-class young men to take a pride in physical labour. Wilde, although known for his physical laziness, nevertheless joined this work-party under the influence of Ruskin. A more significant and lasting influence, though, was Pater. In *The Renaissance,* published in 1873, a year before Wilde's arrival at Oxford, Pater declared himself an atheist, spoke of modern human nature as largely evil, found a strange beauty in evil, and urged that this life should be lived as completely and fully as possible, since it is short and is the only life we have. A shy and retiring man, Pater asserted that the highest pleasure is to be found in art. Many of the young men who read his book, however, misunderstood him, and felt that he was advocating a life of sensations. *The Renaissance* was to remain Wilde's favourite book throughout most of his life.

In 1875 Wilde went on a tour of Italy, and in 1877 he visited Greece. In 1878 he received a degree in classics with first-class honours from Oxford. His success as a student shows very clearly that, despite his affectations, he was a brilliant and hard-working young man. His education accounts for the many classical references in his works. During his years at Oxford, moreover, he began to produce poetry, and his poem 'Ravenna' won the Newdigate Prize in 1878.

The year 1879 marks another change in Wilde's life, for in that year he went to live in London. Almost immediately he became a famous figure, and within two years his fame had become so widespread that he accepted an invitation to go on a year-long lecture tour in the USA. This fame was not the result of any literary achievements. In 1881, Wilde published a volume of poetry which was considered mediocre, and rightly so, since most of the poems in it are poor imitations. Because of the many friendships he had formed at Oxford, where the undergraduates came mostly from the upper-classes, Wilde was able to enter this society with relative ease, and his incomparable wit immediately made him one of its most celebrated members. English upper-class society of that time formed a separate group, and many of its members lived a life of gaiety, splendour, balls, and dinner parties. The activities of those people were of great interest to the general public and were regularly reported in the press, much as the goings-on of film and TV stars are reported today. And because of his social reputation, by the time he was twenty-seven, much of Europe and the USA had heard of Oscar Wilde.

But Wilde was not simply a charming wit in those days. He was also an apostle of the doctrine of aestheticism, which preached to the duty-obsessed Victorians that the pursuit and enjoyment of beauty was the chief purpose of life. Wilde declared that the highest beauty manifests itself in art, but he considered that everything created by human beings was a kind of art. He felt that dress, for instance, is of supreme importance, for the human body is like an empty canvas and clothes are like the paint we use to draw a picture on this canvas. The fully clothed human body, then, is a work of art, and we should strive to make ourselves as beautiful as possible through the way we dress. We should also take great care to build beautiful homes and to make sure that their interior decoration is aesthetically pleasing. Inevitably, such a doctrine was ridiculed by many people, but it caught the attention of the middle-classes, who listened eagerly, if amusedly, to what Wilde had to say.

The turning point

After his return from America in 1883, Wilde fell in love with a very attractive and gentle young woman, Constance Lloyd, and the two got married later that same year. She bore him two sons, the first in 1885, the second in 1886. For a while, he was happily married and very much in love with Connie, but there was latent in him a tendency towards homosexuality. It is possible, though by no means definite, that he had had some mild homosexual experiences while at Oxford. At any rate, his first known homosexual contact occurred late in 1886, at the age of thirty-two, when he was seduced by Robert Ross, a young man fifteen years his junior. From that time on, his history is one of steadily increasing homosexual involvement until he was exposed and imprisoned in 1895.

Homosexual contact sharpened Wilde's sense of evil and strengthened his ability to handle this theme in literature. After 1886, his literary output increased a great deal in quantity and became much better in quality. Strangely enough, the first product of the post-homosexual Wilde was a series of fairy tales, written between 1886 and 1889. These stories deal with the serious themes of innocence, evil, and suffering, but within a delightful fairy-tale framework. They constitute Wilde's attempt to fight the homosexual urge and remain in a childlike world of innocence – the world of his two sons Cyril and Vyvyan. Some of those tales, such as 'Lord Arthur Savile's Crime' and 'The Canterville Ghost', are quite famous and still entertain both children and adults today.

Along with the fairy tales, Wilde wrote a considerable amount of criticism. In one of his critical essays, *Pen, Pencil and Poison* (1889), he speaks of the excellent effect that crime had on the art of the poisoner Thomas Wainewright. Since homosexuality was considered a crime punishable by law in Victorian England, it is easy to connect Wilde with Wainewright and to see Wilde as talking indirectly about the effect of sin and crime on his own work. The best essays, however, are *The Decay of Lying* (1889) and *The Critic as Artist* (1890), both of them more complex than their playful, witty style might lead one to assume.

By 1890, it had become evident to Wilde that for him to resist the homosexual urge was futile. He had become progressively more involved homosexually, and his new decision was to yield to the impulse rather than fight it. Both in his art and life, he initiated a new and darker phase. In life, his homosexual activity became more intense. (His wife Constance did not find out that her husband was a practising homosexual until his exposure in 1895). In art, he wrote *The Picture of Dorian Gray* (1890), his only novel and a good one, despite its many imperfections. The book relates the story of Dorian Gray, a handsome young man who wishes for eternal youth and beauty. He gets his wish, and as he grows older it is his picture that shows signs of age while he remains intact. Dorian also decides to follow a life of sensuality and pleasure, moreover, and the sinful acts that scar his soul are also revealed in his picture. Although it is never openly stated in the novel, Dorian's main sin is homosexuality. In the end, Dorian's pursuit of evil beauty ceases to give pleasure and he begins to yearn desperately for his lost innocence. In an attempt to recover this innocence, he stabs his picture. Far from being destroyed, however, the picture returns to its original state of youthfulness and beauty, while Dorian the man ages in a flash and dies. The novel ends with Dorian's servants finding him dead in the attic, with a knife sticking in his heart. It is only with great difficulty that they recognise the aged corpse as that of their master.

Wilde's view of human nature in *Dorian Gray* is a simple one: he regarded it as grey, a mixture of good and evil. Despite its apparently moral ending, the novel created an uproar, and Wilde was attacked in the press. His first great success did not come until 1892, with the production of his play, *Lady Windermere's Fan.* In a very real sense, the play is a joke on the Victorian public, since it repeats the basic theme of Wilde's novel that human nature is grey. Lady Windermere, a Puritan, discovers in the course of the action that she has a good deal of badness in her. Mrs Erlynne, on the other hand, who is reputedly all bad, finds out that there is a hard core of goodness within herself. The play is a light social comedy full of sparkling wit, and it lacks the dark, sinister atmosphere of *Dorian Gray*. It proved very popular on the London stage.

Lady Windermere's Fan was followed by *A Woman of No Importance* (produced in 1893) and *An Ideal Husband* (produced in 1895). The three plays, all successful, turned Wilde into a famous playwright. Beneath their deceptive conventional framework, they deal with the theme of human evil. The public, however, not understanding the real meaning of the plays and fascinated by their epigrammatic wit, applauded; so that when Wilde sat down to write *The Importance of Being Earnest*, he did so from a position of fame and popularity.

The Importance of Being Earnest is Wilde's funniest and most attractive play, one of the masterpieces of comedy. Written in 1894 while he was on vacation in Brighton, it was first conceived as a four-act play. It proved too long for the stage, however, so Wilde cut parts of it, strengthened it, and recast it as a three-act play. It is the second, shorter version which we read today, although the first version was discovered and published many years ago. *The Importance of*

Being Earnest is a farce, taking us into the realm of absurdity in an attempt to recover a lost innocence. Through laughter, it tries to purge us of sin and evil. It is the only one of Wilde's plays that has not caused much disagreement among his modern-day readers and viewers: practically everyone agrees that it is perfect or nearly so. Ever since its first production in 1895, it has held the stage easily, delighting generation after generation of viewers.

One play that was never produced in England in Wilde's lifetime is *Salomé* (1893; 1894), his darkest and most terrifying work. Written originally in French in 1891, it was banned from the English stage by the Lord Chamberlain. An anti-Christian play, it presents the prophet Jokanaan (John the Baptist) as a person who has repressed his nature. The cruel and sexually perverse Salomé, on the other hand, is a symbol of human nature. In the final decade of the nineteenth century, many people believed that the appearance of the Antichrist was imminent. Wilde in *Salomé* presents himself as the Antichrist, preaching that human nature is totally and irredeemably evil. *Salomé* is Wilde's most evil and terrible work, and its interpretation of human nature is wholly satanic.

In 1891 Wilde met and formed an association with Lord Alfred Douglas, who from that time on became his chief homosexual love. Douglas's father, however, was the Marquess of Queensberry, a highly eccentric and violent man, who soon began a campaign of threats and scandal against Wilde, in an attempt to rescue his son from his influence. (In fact, it was more truthfully Wilde who had fallen under the influence of the younger but more corrupt Alfred). In 1895, Wilde finally decided to take action against Queensberry, and he imprudently sued him for criminal libel. At the trial, Wilde's homosexual activity was exposed, Queensberry was acquitted, and Wilde was placed under arrest. He was then tried on charges of homosexuality. At the first trial the jury disagreed, but at the second he was found guilty and given the maximum sentence of two years' imprisonment with hard labour.

The end

His prison years, spent mostly in Reading Gaol, were difficult and psychologically destructive ones. In 1897 and while in prison, he wrote *De Profundis,* which is both a literary document and a letter to Lord Alfred Douglas. After his release, he wrote *The Ballad of Reading Gaol* (1895), a good poem but flawed. This was to be his last literary production, however, for he discovered that prison had permanently destroyed his ability to write. Soon after his release, and finding himself a shunned man in England, he assumed the name

Sebastian Melmoth and departed for the Continent, where he spent the last three years of his life, a lonely and broken man. He died in Paris in November 1900, at the age of forty-six. Throughout his mature literary career, Wilde consciously wrote literature that he wished to be regarded as the culmination of nineteenth-century literary history. It is therefore fitting that he died at the turn of the century.

The history of nineteenth-century British drama

In one significant way, however, Wilde's literature was not the end of the nineteenth-century impulse but the beginning of a twentieth-century one. Throughout the nineteenth century, the English theatre was in a state of decline and decay, but in the 1890s what was called the 'new drama' appeared. The chief apostles of this movement which revivified the English theatre were George Bernard Shaw and Oscar Wilde.

In the nineteenth century, a special type of drama referred to as melodrama had come more and more to dominate the English stage. Melodramas were intended for lower-class people without much education, who lived in crowded, unattractive homes and worked long hours. These were the people who provided the basic audience for the playwrights. When such people did have free evenings to go to the theatre, they were not in the mood for intellectual entertainment. They wanted something exciting, emotional, funny, and this is what the melodramas of the period gave them. The main characteristics of melodrama are the following: (*i*) simple, easy dialogue, though pretentious and seldom realistic. (*ii*) visual variety; there were usually a number of short scenes per act, with many changes of setting. (*iii*) much music and sound effects for emotional stimulation. (*iv*) stiff, flimsy, unconvincing pasteboard characters; usually, a character had simply one basic characteristic that identified him, such as drunkenness, courage, villainy, purity. (*v*) accidental and unconvincing appearances, sudden reversals, suspense, and excitement were preferable to probability.

The first departure from this crude type of melodrama came with the plays of T.W. Robertson. Such plays of his as *Society* (1865), *Caste* (1867), and *School* (1869) displayed some serious intellectual content, and characters were fuller and more rounded. Then came the plays of Henry Arthur Jones and A.W. Pinero. Pinero wrote such plays as *The Silver King* (1882) and *Saints and Sinners* (1884), while Jones's plays included *The Profligate* (1889) and *The Second Mrs Tanqueray* (1893).

These playwrights, however, simply paved the way for Shaw and Wilde. Moreover, by the final decades of the century, the middle and upper-classes had begun to frequent the theatres, and they wanted a more sophisticated type of drama. The plays of Shaw and Wilde, though they owe much to the conventions of melodrama, present us with many-sided and convincing characters. Much more significant, though, is that they have a good deal of intellectual content. Indeed, the main difference between melodrama and the New Drama is that, while the former is unintellectual, the latter is a drama of ideas.

The Importance of Being Earnest – a unique play of its kind in English literature – cannot be considered a drama of ideas despite the fact that it does have intellectual content. Nevertheless, in its break with melodrama and its almost total originality, it is very definitely part of the late nineteenth-century revival of the drama. It stands today as the best play that Great Britain produced in the nineteenth century.

A note on the text

Although produced on the London stage in 1895, *The Importance of Being Earnest* was not published until 1899, when Leonard Smithers brought out the first edition in London. This was the three-act version, which Wilde rightly considered to be the stronger one. Since then, the play has been published many times and translated into many languages. The 1899 edition is the authoritative text on which all subsequent editions have been based.

Part 2

Summaries
of THE IMPORTANCE OF
BEING EARNEST

The characters

It is best to begin a summary of *The Importance of Being Earnest* by introducing, very briefly, the characters in the play and outlining their roles.

John (Jack) Worthing, J.P.

One of the main characters in the play, he has a double identity. In the country, where he has an estate and is in charge of the upbringing of Cecily Cardew, he is the respectable Jack Worthing, a very serious and upright young man (Jack is the diminutive of John, just as Algy is the diminutive of Algernon). He makes frequent trips to London, however, where he assumes the name of Ernest Worthing and pursues a life of pleasure. In the play, he is in love with Gwendolen Fairfax and seeks her hand in marriage.

Algernon Moncrieff

Another main character in the play, he lives in London, where he is constantly watched over by his ultra-respectable aunt, Lady Bracknell. However, he has invented a permanent invalid friend, Bunbury, who lives in the country. In the play, he goes 'Bunburying' under the name of Ernest Worthing, Jack's fictitious wicked younger brother, in order to meet Cecily Cardew, with whom he falls immediately in love and to whom he proposes marriage.

The Hon. Gwendolen Fairfax

The daughter of Lady Bracknell, she is an aristocrat and a beautiful young girl. She is in love with Jack Worthing in the play, and wishes to marry him despite her mother's strong disapproval. She knows him, however, under the assumed name of Ernest Worthing. In keeping with the nonsensical nature of the play, one of Jack's chief attractions for Gwendolen is his assumed name – Ernest – without which she would refuse to marry him.

Cecily Cardew

Jack's beautiful eighteen-year-old ward. She lives in the country and is tutored by Miss Prism. She nurses a secret love for Jack's nonexistent brother Ernest, mainly because of his name and his wicked reputation. When Algernon appears under the assumed name and identity of Ernest Worthing, she sees him as her prospective husband, but soon discovers that his real name is not Ernest.

Lady Bracknell

Gwendolen's mother and Algy's aunt, she is a member of the British aristocracy. Her chief passion in life is to maintain and strengthen her superior social position. Thus, she is intent on making a good match for her daughter, and also interferes in Algy's matrimonial plans. She strongly opposes the marriage of Gwendolen and Jack in the play.

Reverend Canon Chasuble, D.D.

The Rector of Jack's country parish, he strictly follows the rules of the Primitive Church as regards matrimony, and is therefore a celibate. However, he has a nonsensical passion for the unattractive Miss Prism. He represses this passion, but it shows nevertheless. In the play, he undertakes to christen both Jack and Algy.

Miss Prism

A humourless middle-aged woman, she is Cecily Cardew's governess. She disapproves of Cecily's playfulness and vivaciousness, and would like her to be serious and apply herself to the study of German grammar and similar subjects for the sake of 'improving' herself. Miss Prism, moreover, is very interested in Canon Chasuble, and tries in the play to persuade him to marry her.

Lane

A minor character in the play, he is Algernon's devoted manservant.

Merriman

Another minor character, he is Jack's butler.

The student should remember that **Mr Bunbury** and **Ernest Worthing** are not actual characters in the play. Bunbury is a fictional character invented by Algernon for the sake of escaping periodically into the country. Ernest Worthing is a fictional name and identity invented by Jack. Algy later assumes this name and identity when he goes to visit Jack at his country home.

A general summary

Act I

Jack Worthing, under the assumed name of Ernest Worthing, has arrived in London in order to propose to Gwendolen Fairfax, and he goes to see his friend, Algernon Moncrieff, who lives in a luxurious flat. However, Jack had lost a cigarette case previously and Algy has found it. The cigarette case leads Algy to discover that Jack has a double identity: he is Ernest in the city and Jack in the country. Jack explains that, in order to leave his country home whenever he wishes, he has invented a fictitious wicked younger brother named Ernest, who lives in London and often gets into so much trouble that he has to dash off to rescue him. Jack's many trips to London are for the sake of pleasure. It turns out that Algy, too, leads a double life. Algy has invented a friend called Bunbury who resides in the country and is a permanent invalid. Because of Bunbury, Algy is able to go on a pleasure trip to the country whenever he wishes.

The doorbell rings, and Lady Bracknell and her daughter Gwendolen enter. Algy was expecting them, and had prepared a tray of cucumber sandwiches for Lady Bracknell but has eaten it all before her arrival. When Algy and his aunt leave the room momentarily, Jack seizes the opportunity to confess to Gwendolen that he passionately adores her. He is amazed to learn that she too is deeply in love with him, but she goes on to say that the main reason she loves him is because his name is Ernest. After deciding privately to christen himself Ernest at once, Jack proposes to Gwendolen and she accepts him. While he is still on his knees, however, Lady Bracknell re-enters and insists on subjecting him to a thorough questioning about his wealth and social position. At first, Jack's answers are satisfactory, but when she asks him about his parents, he admits that he does not know who they are. Jack explains that he was found in a handbag by a Mr Thomas Cardew in a cloakroom at Victoria Station, and was given the name Worthing because Mr Cardew happened to have a first-class ticket for Worthing in his pocket at the time. Lady Bracknell is shocked by this information and absolutely forbids any engagement between Jack and Gwendolen until Jack has produced at least one satisfactory parent. Gwendolen, on the other hand, is undeterred by Jack's story of his origin, for she finds the fascination of the name Ernest irresistible. She asks for and obtains Jack's country address. Algy, listening in the background, jots the address down on his shirt-cuff. The act ends with Algy preparing to go on a 'Bunbury' to Jack's country home in order to meet Cecily Cardew, of whose existence he has learnt.

Act II

The scene opens in the garden of Jack's country home, where Cecily is with her governess, Miss Prism. Miss Prism is trying to persuade Cecily to concentrate on her studies, but Cecily is inattentive. Dr Chasuble soon appears, and Miss Prism goes for a walk with him. The butler Merriman comes into the garden and announces the arrival of Mr Ernest Worthing. Actually, the person who has arrived is Algernon, who has assumed the name and identity of Jack's fictitious brother in order to meet Cecily. They do meet and converse for a while, then they enter the house. Immediately after that, Miss Prism and Dr Chasuble return to the garden. Presently, Jack enters, dressed completely in black, and sadly announces that his brother died in Paris the night before. The situation, of course, is hilarious, and it becomes even more so when Cecily reemerges from the house and joyfully announces to Jack that his brother Ernest is in the dining-room! Algy appears, and although Jack is furious with him, Cecily insists on a reconciliation between the two 'brothers'. Left alone with Algy, Jack demands his immediate return to London. Algy, however, has fallen in love with Cecily. Then follows a long and hilarious conversation between Algy and Cecily, during which he proposes marriage and discovers that he has already been engaged to her for three whole months! Cecily, it seems, fell in love with him when she learned how wicked he was. Moreover, she has always had a girlish dream of loving someone by the name of Ernest. When Algy learns this, he runs off to see Dr Chasuble about being rechristened Ernest.

Merriman enters and announces the presence of Miss Gwendolen Fairfax, who has come to see Mr Worthing on very important business. Cecily receives Gwendolen, and the two girls discover during their conversation that they are both engaged to Mr Ernest Worthing. The return of Jack and Algernon, however, exposes the truth: Cecily reveals Jack's real identity and Gwendolen unmasks Algy. The girls, who only a moment ago had been at each other's throats, cling together for comfort and withdraw scornfully into the house, while the men remain in the garden and argue. The act ends with Jack and Algy nonsensically quarrelling over which of them is to eat a dish of muffins the girls had left behind.

Act III

The act begins in the morning-room of Jack's country house, with Cecily and Gwendolen longing for a reconciliation with their respective lovers. Jack and Algy soon enter, and a reconciliation takes place quite easily. The final obstacle is removed when the two men announce that they are going to be rechristened Ernest that very afternoon. But Lady Bracknell appears unexpectedly, absolutely forbids Gwendolen to marry Jack, then begins to subject him to a severe questioning about Algy's fiancée. When it turns out that Cecily has approximately £130,000 in the Funds, Lady Bracknell's attitude changes very dramatically, and she quickly consents to the marriage of Cecily and Algy. Jack, however, who is Cecily's guardian, forbids the marriage unless Lady Bracknell also agrees that he should marry Gwendolen. This she refuses to do, and the situation looks quite hopeless until Dr Chasuble arrives. He mentions Miss Prism's name, and Lady Bracknell suddenly becomes very excited and insists on meeting her. It turns out that about twenty years earlier Miss Prism had been the governess of Lady Bracknell's sister and had been entrusted with a baby, which she had lost. She confesses that she had accidentally placed the baby in a black leather handbag, which she had left in the cloakroom at Victoria Station. Jack produces the handbag in which he was found, and Prism recognises it as the one she had mislaid. Thus, Jack's parentage is discovered. He turns out to be Algy's elder brother, the son of Lady Bracknell's sister and General Ernest John Moncrieff. It also emerges that his name is really Ernest, after all. All obstacles to marriage have now been overcome, and the play ends with Jack embracing Gwendolen and Algy embracing Cecily. Dr Chasuble also rejects his former views on celibacy and embraces Miss Prism.

Detailed summaries

Act I

The opening scene is laid in the luxurious, artistically furnished morning-room of Algernon Moncrieff's flat in Half-Moon Street, London. Lane, Algernon's manservant, is arranging afternoon tea on the table while the sound of a piano drifts in from the adjoining room.

After the music has ceased, Algernon Moncrieff enters. He makes some remarks about his not playing the piano accurately but achieving wonderful expression, then asks Lane if he has prepared the cucumber sandwiches for Lady Bracknell, whom he is expecting. Lane brings him the sandwiches. Algernon inspects them, then eats two and sits down on the sofa. He asks Lane about the eight bottles of champagne that were consumed a few days previously, and asks why it is that at a bachelor's home the servants invariably drink the champagne. Lane, calm and unperturbed, gives the superior quality of the wine as the reason.

Jack Worthing enters, and is announced by Lane as 'Mr Ernest Worthing'. Algernon greets him warmly. Jack has come up to London from his country home, which he says is in Shropshire, for the sake of amusing himself. He is perfectly delighted to learn that Lady Bracknell and her daughter Gwendolen Fairfax are coming to visit Algy. When Algy declares that Lady Bracknell is going to be displeased to find him there, because he flirts outrageously with Gwendolen, 'Ernest' announces that he is in London for the express purpose of proposing marriage to Gwendolen.

As her cousin, however, Algernon – who continues to eat cucumber sandwiches all the time – refuses to give his consent until Jack clears up the little matter of Cecily. 'Cecily!' Jack denies knowing anyone by that name. However, Jack had lost a cigarette case in Algy's flat and Algy had found it. Lane brings the cigarette case, but Algy refuses to give it to Jack since he has asserted that he does not know anyone by the name of Cecily, and the cigarette case has the name 'Cecily' inscribed in it. Jack impatiently says that Cecily is his aunt, a charming old lady who lives at Tunbridge Wells. But Algy is dissatisfied, and asks why the inscription reads 'From little Cecily with her fondest love'. Jack replies that 'some aunts are tall, some aunts are not tall. That is a matter that surely an aunt may be allowed to decide for herself'. But why does Cecily call him uncle? Algy reads the entire inscription: 'From little Cecily, with her fondest love to her dear Uncle Jack.' Besides, since his name is Ernest, not Jack, the cigarette case cannot possibly belong to him. Algy even produces one of Jack's visiting-cards as proof that his name is Ernest. Finding himself trapped, Jack explains that he is called Jack in the country and Ernest in town. Algy says that he has long suspected Jack of being a confirmed 'Bunburyist', and he offers to explain what that term means after Jack has told him all about Cecily.

After his cigarette case has been returned to him, Jack explains that his foster-father, Mr Thomas Cardew, had appointed him in his will guardian to his granddaughter, Miss Cecily Cardew:

When one is placed in the position of guardian, one has to adopt a very high moral tone on all subjects. It's one's duty to do so. And as a high moral tone can hardly be said to conduce very much to either one's health or one's happiness, in order to get up to town I have always pretended to have a younger brother of the name of Ernest, who lives in the Albany, and gets into the most dreadful scrapes.

Algy calls Jack one of the most advanced 'Bunburyists' he knows, then explains that he – Algy – has invented an invaluable permanent invalid, Bunbury, and that this enables him to go on pleasure trips in the country whenever he wishes.

Jack, however, insists that he is not a 'Bunburyist', and that if Gwendolen accepts him, he is going to kill off his fictitious brother Ernest. Indeed, he adds, he may kill him off anyway, as Cecily is becoming somewhat too interested in him. He advises Algy to do the same with Bunbury, but Algy replies that nothing could induce him to commit such an act.

Algy coolly informs Jack that he plans to dine with him that night at Willis's, as his guest. Lady Bracknell has invited him to dinner at her home, he explains, but he has a strong suspicion that she will place him next to Mary Farquhar, who always flirts with her own husband across the dinner-table! Besides, he dined with his Aunt Augusta (Lady Bracknell) on Monday, 'and once a week is quite enough to dine with one's own relations'. Jack at first refuses to invite Algy, but succumbs when the latter promises to keep his Aunt Augusta out of the way for ten minutes, so that Jack can be alone with Gwendolen.

The sound of an electric bell is heard, then Lane enters and announces Lady Bracknell and Miss Fairfax. They come in, and Algy greets his aunt while Jack pays extravagant compliments to Gwendolen, then sits down with her in the corner. Lady Bracknell moves to the tea-table for a cup of tea and some cucumber sandwiches. Algy, picking up the empty cucumber-plate in horror, asks Lane why there are no cucumber sandwiches, since he ordered them especially. The answer, of course, is that Algy ate them all! Lane calmly and loyally covers up for his master, declaring that there were no cucumbers on the market, not even for ready money. Algy apologises to his aunt, who declares that she has a treat for him – she wants him to come to dinner that night, and announces that she is going to seat him next to Mary Farquhar, who is a delightful woman and very attentive to her husband!

Algy declines the invitation because, he says, he has received a telegram that his friend Bunbury is very ill again, and he must go to his side. Lady Bracknell is quite irritated, and states that 'it is high time that Mr Bunbury made up his mind whether he was going to live or to die'. She then requests that Algy ask Bunbury to kindly not have a relapse on Saturday, since she needs Algy to arrange the music for her last reception of the season. Algy promises, on Bunbury's behalf, that Bunbury will be all right on Saturday, then invites Lady Bracknell to the next room to discuss the music programme. Lady Bracknell orders her daughter to follow her, and Gwendolen replies, 'Certainly, mamma' – but remains behind!

Jack and Gwendolen are now alone, and he nervously begins a conversation about the weather. Gwendolen interrupts impatiently, asking him to get to the point, especially since her mother has an irritating way of coming back suddenly into a room. Jack timidly declares his love for Gwendolen, and immediately discovers that she too is very much in love with him. 'Even before I met you I was far from indifferent to you,' she says to the amazed Jack. This is because her 'ideal has always been to love someone of the name of Ernest. There is something in that name that inspires absolute confidence'. Jack asks if she would still love him if his name were, for instance – Jack. No, comes the reply. Realising that he must change his name at once, he blurts out: 'Gwendolen, I must get christened at once – I mean we must get married at once. There is no time to be lost.' Gwendolen insists on a formal proposal. Jack goes on his knees and asks her to marry him, and she accepts, chiding him for having taken such a long time to propose.

Suddenly, Lady Bracknell enters and finds Jack in a 'semi-recumbent posture'. Gwendolen announces to her mother that she and Jack are engaged, but Lady Bracknell firmly orders her to go to the carriage, then brings out a notebook and pencil from her pocket, orders Jack to sit down, and begins to subject him to a string of questions. She informs Jack that he is not on her list of eligible young men – the same list as the Duchess of Bolton's – but that she is prepared to enter his name if his answers are satisfactory. We learn from the interrogation that Jack smokes, is twenty-nine, has an income of between £7,000 and £8,000 a year from investments, owns a country house with some land attached to it, owns a town house in Belgrave Square, which is let by the year to Lady Bloxham, and is a Liberal Unionist. Lady Bracknell finds all those answers quite satisfactory, although she is displeased that Jack's London house is on the un-fashionable side of Belgrave Square.

When Lady Bracknell begins to question Jack about his parents, however, he is forced to admit that he does not know who they are. He explains that he was found by the late Mr Thomas Cardew in the cloakroom at Victoria Station. Mr Cardew, he says, found him in a somewhat large, black leather handbag with handles to it, and gave him the name of Worthing because he happened to have a first-class ticket for Worthing in his pocket at the time. Lady Bracknell is shocked by this information, and states haughtily: 'To be born, or at any rate bred, in a hand-bag, whether it had handles or not, seems to me to display a contempt for the ordinary decencies of family life that remind one of the worst excesses of the French Revolution.' At any rate, it can 'hardly be regarded as an assured basis for a recognised position in good society'. She advises Jack to produce at least one parent before the end of the season, and when Jack replies that he can produce the handbag, she retorts that Lord Bracknell and herself can hardly allow their only daughter to 'form an alliance with a parcel', then sweeps out in majestic indignation.

From the other room Algy, assuming that all had gone well, strikes up the Wedding March. Jack goes to the door and furiously orders him to stop. Algy enters cheerily and learns the sad news. Jack calls Lady Bracknell a Gorgon, then quickly apologises to Algy for abusing his aunt before him. Algy, however, replies that he loves to hear his relatives abused. He asks if Jack has told Gwendolen about his double identity, but Jack's response is that 'the truth isn't quite the sort of thing one tells to a nice, sweet, refined girl. What extraordinary ideas you have about the way to behave to a woman'. Jack then declares that he is going to get rid of his fictitious brother Ernest – he is going to announce that Ernest has died in Paris of a severe chill. Algy inquires how this will affect Cecily, then reminds Jack that it is time for them to dress for dinner. Algy, much to Jack's irritation, has not forgotten that he is to be Jack's guest at dinner that night.

Lane enters, announces Miss Fairfax, then withdraws. Gwendolen comes in hurriedly and asks Algy to turn his back, as 'I have something very particular to say to Mr Worthing'. She then informs Jack that she has found the story of his origin, as related to her by her mother, very romantic, that nothing can alter her eternal devotion to him, and that his name – Ernest – fascinates her irresistibly. Though her mother may be able to prevent their marriage, she will never be able to kill her love for him. She asks for his country address, and he gives it to her: 'The Manor House, Woolton, Hertfordshire'. In the background Algy, who has been carefully listening, smiles and writes the address on his shirt-cuff.

Jack offers to see Gwendolen to her carriage, and the two walk out. Algernon informs Lane, who has entered, that he plans to go 'Bunburying' the next day and asks him to prepare his suits for him. Jack re-enters, and Algy hints to him that he is planning a 'Bunbury' and declares that he loves scrapes. Jack looks at him indignantly, and leaves the room. The act ends with Algernon lighting a cigarette and smiling to himself as he reads his shirt-cuff.

NOTES AND GLOSSARY:

Half-Moon Street: a street in Mayfair, at that time the most fashionable part of London. The fact that Algernon's flat is in

	Mayfair suggests that he is a member of the upper-classes, and this impression is reinforced by the luxurious furniture and the presence of a 'morning-room', which implies that there is also a more formal drawing-room. The flat also has an electric bell, a clear indication at that time that it is ultra-modern
Liberal Unionist:	a person belonging to the party formed by those Liberals who opposed the efforts of Gladstone, the prime minister, to give Home Rule to Ireland. The fact that Jack is a Liberal Unionist, and that Lady Bracknell approves of this, is part of the fun in the play. Wilde naturally wished to see his native Ireland secure Home Rule
Gorgon:	in Greek mythology, the Gorgons were three frightful sisters whose heads had hissing snakes instead of hair, and who had claws, huge teeth, and wings. The most famous of them was Medusa, whose sight turned men to stone

Act II

This act is set entirely in the garden of Jack's country house. A flight of grey stone steps leads up to the house. The time of year is July and the garden is in full bloom. As the curtain rises, there are chairs, and a table covered with books, under a large yew tree. Miss Prism, Cecily Cardew's governess, is seated at the table, while Cecily is at the back of the stage watering flowers.

The act begins with Miss Prism calling to Cecily to leave the watering of the flowers to the gardener and give herself to the pursuit of intellectual pleasures, such as the German lesson which awaits her. Cecily complains that she doesn't like German, and that she always looks plain after her German lesson. Miss Prism, however, stresses that Cecily's guardian is very anxious that she should improve herself in every way, and that, as usual, he laid particular stress on her German before leaving for town. Cecily retorts that her dear Uncle Jack is so serious that sometimes she thinks he cannot be quite well, but Miss Prism sternly defends Jack's seriousness and says that she knows no one who has a higher sense of duty and responsibility. Then the conversation turns to Jack's wicked brother Ernest, and Cecily wishes that Jack would allow Ernest to come to their country house for a visit sometime, adding that Miss Prism may have a good influence over him, for she knows German and geology! Miss Prism doubts that even she can reform Ernest, and adds that she disapproves of the modern mania of turning bad people into good people at a moment's notice. She then mentions that she wrote a three-volume novel once, and Cecily hopes that it did not end happily, for novels that end happily depress her very much. Miss Prism declares that 'the good ended happily, and the bad unhappily. That is what Fiction means'. Unfortunately, she adds, her novel was never published, for the manuscript was abandoned.

Dr Chasuble enters, and Miss Prism greets him very warmly. Cecily, noticing that her governess is attracted to the Rector, quickly states that Miss Prism has a headache, and that a short stroll with Dr Chasuble would do her much good. Miss Prism objects that she did not mention anything about a headache, and Dr Chasuble hopes that Cecily has not been inattentive to her studies. She admits that she has, and the Rector observes that this is strange, for were he fortunate enough to be Miss Prism's pupil, he 'would hang upon her lips'. Miss Prism glares, and Dr Chasuble, realising that his words have a double meaning, becomes very embarrassed and adds immediately that he spoke metaphorically and that his metaphor was drawn from bees. He then observes that he must not disturb Egeria and her pupil any longer, and when Miss Prism reminds him, with some puzzlement, that her name is Laetitia, he says that he was merely making a classical allusion. Miss Prism decides to have a stroll with Dr Chasuble, and he offers to walk with her as far as the schools and back. She instructs Cecily to read her political economy by herself, then goes down the garden with the Rector. As soon as they are gone, Cecily picks up the books and throws them back on the table, calling them horrid.

Merriman, the butler, enters and announces 'Mr Ernest Worthing', who has arrived with his luggage. Cecily asks him to bring Mr Worthing to her, and Algernon enters, very gay and debonair. We realise at once that Algy is on a 'Bunbury' and has assumed the name and identity of Jack's fictitious brother Ernest, but Cecily, of course, knows nothing of this, for she has never met 'Ernest'. Algy calls her 'my little cousin Cecily', but when Cecily calls him 'my wicked cousin Ernest', Algy denies that he is really wicked. Cecily is so disappointed by this statement that Algy, in amazement, is forced to withdraw it and admit that he has in fact been very bad. Cecily then informs him that her Uncle Jack won't be back till Monday afternoon, and 'Ernest' pretends to be disappointed and says that he has to leave on Monday morning. But Jack wants to talk to him about his emigrating to Australia, Cecily tells him. 'He has gone up to buy your outfit.' Algy refuses to emigrate to Australia and asks Cecily to reform him instead. When she replies that she hasn't time that afternoon, he decides to reform himself, then declares that he is hungry. She invites him into the house for some food, and on the way in, he compares her to a pink rose and informs her that she is the prettiest girl he has ever seen.

Cecily and Algernon pass into the house. Miss Prism and Dr Chasuble return, engaged in deep conversation. Miss Prism is trying to convince the Rector that he should get married; she suggests a mature woman for him, and argues that a man converts himself into a permanent public temptation by remaining single. Chasuble, however, declares that both the doctrine and the practice of the Primitive Church was clearly against marriage.

The conversation is interrupted by the slow entrance of Jack from the back of the garden. He is in deepest mourning, and is dressed in black from head to toe, with a black crepe hatband and black gloves. In a tragic and sorrowful manner, he announces the untimely death of his brother. Ernest, he explains, died suddenly the previous night of a severe chill in Paris, where – according to his own wish – he is going to be buried. Miss Prism declares harshly that he got exactly what he deserved, but Dr Chasuble offers his sincere condolence. He promises to mention this personal tragedy on Sunday, during his sermon on the meaning of the manna in the wilderness, which, he says, 'can be adapted to almost any occasion, joyful, or, as in the present case, distressing'. Chasuble recounts all the occasions when he preached this sermon, mentioning also christenings, and Jack asks him if he knows how to christen satisfactorily. The Canon says yes, and Jack asks to be christened that same afternoon, 'if you have nothing else to do'. When Chasuble objects that surely Jack has already been christened, Jack answers that he doesn't remember anything about it! They agree to hold the ceremony at half-past five. The Canon assures Jack there will be no immersion. A sprinkling is all that is necessary – or advisable, since the weather is so changeable!

Suddenly, Cecily emerges from the house and goes towards Jack. He kisses her brow in a melancholy manner, only to hear her announce that his brother Ernest is in the dining-room! Jack declares that the very idea is absurd, since he hasn't got a brother, but Cecily runs back into the house and returns with Algernon. Algy begins to apologise to his 'brother John' for his sinful life, promises to lead a better life in the future, and offers his hand. Jack glares at him and refuses to shake hands. Cecily is quite upset, however, and insists on a reconciliation. For her sake, Jack finally yields and shakes Algy's hand. Cecily, her 'little task of reconciliation' over, withdraws with Dr Chasuble and Miss Prism, leaving the two men together. Jack calls Algy a scoundrel and orders him to leave at once. Merriman enters and announces that he has placed 'Mr Ernest's' things in the room next to Jack's, and Algy declares that he cannot stay for more than a week. Furious, Jack asks Merriman to order the dogcart at once, for 'Mr Ernest has been suddenly called back to town'. Algy refuses to depart leaving Jack in a state of mourning, however, for that would be very unkind. He agrees to leave, though, if Jack will change his black clothes.

Jack goes into the house to change, and Cecily enters at the back of the garden and begins to water the flowers. Algy goes over to her and tells her that Jack is sending him away, then Merriman appears and announces the arrival of the dogcart. Cecily asks the dogcart to wait for a few minutes, and Algy, seizing the opportunity, tells her that he has found her to be 'in every way the visible personification of absolute perfection'. She is quite delighted by this, and starts copying his remarks into her diary! When she reaches 'absolute perfection', she allows him to go on. Algy is somewhat taken aback, but recovers and declares that her beauty is beyond compare and that he loves her 'wildly, passionately, devotedly, hopelessly'. Once again, however, her reaction surprises Algy, for she calmly objects to 'hopelessly' as not making much sense.

Merriman re-enters and announces that the dogcart is waiting, but Algy says it should come back a week later, at the same hour. The butler withdraws, and Algy, wasting no time, asks Cecily to marry him. 'Of course', comes the reply, since they have been engaged for the last three months. When he asks how they became engaged, she explains that, ever since her uncle confessed to them that he has a wicked younger brother, 'Ernest' became the chief topic of conversation between her and Miss Prism. And of course a man who is much talked about is always very attractive, so she fell in love with him. Cecily continues that the engagement was settled on the 14th of February, and shows him the 'dear old tree' under which she accepted him. She also produces a ring and a bangle with a true lovers' knot that she promised him always to wear, then points to the box in which she keeps all his letters. Algy, much bewildered, objects that he never wrote her any letters, and she replies: 'You need hardly remind me of that, Ernest. I remember only too well that I was forced to write all your letters for you. I wrote always three times a week, and sometimes oftener'. She then informs him that their engagement was broken off on the 22nd of March – 'It would hardly have been a really serious engagement if it hadn't been broken off at least once' – but that she forgave him before the week was out.

When Algy seeks assurances that the engagement will not be broken off again, Cecily calms his fears, adding that it was always a girlish dream of hers to love a person by the name of Ernest, a name that 'seems to inspire absolute confidence'. But surely she would still love him if his name were, for instance – Algernon? No! She might respect him and admire his character, but she would not be able to love him. Appreciating the situation, Algy, after asking Cecily if the local Rector is thoroughly experienced in all the rites and ceremonials of the Church, kisses her and dashes off to see Dr Chasuble on most important business – his own christening!

Merriman enters and announces 'a Miss Fairfax to see Mr Worthing' concerning a very important matter. Jack is temporarily absent, so Cecily asks the butler to invite Miss Fairfax into the garden and bring tea. The meeting begins in a friendly manner, and each agrees to call the other by her first name. Gwendolen mentions that her father is Lord Bracknell, but is not surprised that Cecily has not heard of him, since he is entirely unknown outside the family circle. She then asks if Cecily is on a visit at the Manor House, only to learn that she lives there and is Mr Worthing's ward. The news disturbs Gwendolen, who wishes that Cecily 'were fully forty-two and more than usually plain'. Ernest, she says, has a strong upright nature, but 'even men of the noblest possible moral character are extremely susceptible to the influence of the physical charms of others'. Cecily points out that it is not Ernest Worthing but his elder brother Jack who is her guardian. Gwendolen is relieved, despite the fact that she never knew Ernest had a brother. In fact, Cecily adds, she and Ernest are engaged to be married. This announcement brings about a rapid alteration in the situation. Gwendolen rises very politely and announces that it is she who is engaged to Mr Ernest Worthing. Cecily also rises quite politely and shows her diary, in which it is recorded that Ernest proposed to her exactly ten minutes before. Gwendolen replies that she has the prior claim, since Ernest proposed to her the day before at half-past five in the afternoon. Cecily, however, feels that Ernest has clearly changed his mind and that the Gwendolen entanglement is an unfortunate affair with which she will never reproach him after they are married.

The two girls begin to insult one another, but suddenly Merriman and a footman enter, carrying a salver, table cloth, and plate stand. As Merriman lays tea, the girls continue to taunt one another, but in a restrained manner, because of the presence of servants. Gwendolen asks for tea with no sugar and for bread and butter instead of cake, since, she says haughtily, sugar with tea and cake are no longer fashionable in the best houses. Angrily, Cecily places four lumps of sugar in Gwendolen's tea and cuts her a large slice of cake. Gwendolen rises in indignation and warns Cecily not to go too far. Cecily retorts that it seems to her she is trespassing on Gwendolen's valuable time, and that no doubt she has many other calls of a similar character to make in the neighbourhood.

At this explosive moment, Jack enters and, delighted to see Gwendolen, offers to kiss her. She draws back and demands to know if he is engaged to Cecily. 'Of course not!' he says laughingly, and she offers her cheek. Very sweetly, Cecily declares that she knew there was a misunderstanding, and informs Gwendolen that 'the gentleman whose arm is at present around your waist is my dear guardian, Mr John Worthing'. Surprised and shocked, Gwendolen recedes from Jack.

Suddenly, Algernon enters and now the unmasking is completed. Cecily declares that here is Ernest, but when he offers to kiss her, she asks him first to state whether or not he is engaged to Gwendolen. Algy looks round and is very unpleasantly surprised when he sees Gwendolen, but says that, of course, he is not engaged to her. Cecily allows him to kiss her, while Gwendolen points out that 'the gentleman who is now embracing you is my cousin, Mr Algernon Moncrieff'. Cecily breaks away from Algy in horror.

Exposed, Jack and Algy are forced to admit the truth, and Jack explains that there is no such person as Ernest Worthing. The two girls, realising that a gross deception had been practised on both of them, embrace each other in sisterly compassion, then retire into the house with scornful looks.

Jack turns upon Algy and blames him and his absurd 'Bunburying' for what has happened. Algy remains unperturbed, however, and Jack says that his only satisfaction in this whole affair is that Bunbury is now exploded; Algy retorts that Ernest too has been destroyed and that Jack won't be able to use that excuse again to go up to London. Jack says that Algy's conduct towards Cecily was inexcusable, while Algy says the same thing of Jack's conduct towards Gwendolen. Neither considers that the other now has any hope of marriage. In the midst of their argument, Algy begins to eat muffins, an action which infuriates Jack. Algy defends himself by saying that he is eating muffins because he is unhappy. Besides, he adds, he is particularly fond of muffins. Jack takes the muffins from him and begins to eat them himself, since a man may eat his own muffins in his own garden. Algy objects and seizes the muffin-dish from Jack. Jack asks him to leave, but Algy says he cannot possibly leave without having dinner. It would be absurd! Besides, he has made arrangements with Dr Chasuble to be christened at a quarter to six under the name of Ernest. Jack declares that he himself is going to be christened Ernest at half-past five and while there is no evidence that he has been christened before, Algy has already been christened. But that was years and years ago, Algy replies. Besides, the fact that he has been christened before proves that his constitution can stand it, while Jack should not undertake such a dangerous venture if he is not sure he has been christened before. After all, Jack's brother nearly died that same week in Paris of a severe chill. Jack begins to eat muffins again. Algy, objecting that there are only two left, takes them from him. Jack insists that Algy should leave, but Algy replies that he hasn't quite finished his tea yet, and there is still one muffin left. The act ends with Jack groaning and sinking into a chair as Algernon continues to eat.

NOTES AND GLOSSARY:

Egeria: a beautiful nymph who was both the teacher and the lover of King Numa Pompilius, the legendary second king of Rome, who was famous for his great wisdom. Egeria instructed him about forms of worship and inspired the religious reforms he introduced

The Primitive Church: the Christian Church in the centuries immediately following the death of Christ

Canon Chasuble, D.D.: he is Dr Chasuble because he holds a Doctorate in Divinity (D.D.). He is also attached to a cathedral as a member of the Bishop's counsel, and is thus Canon Chasuble. These titles indicate his high rank in the Church

Act III

This act, the shortest in the play, is set entirely in the morning-room of the Manor House, Jack's country home. It begins with Gwendolen and Cecily at the window, looking out into the garden and wondering if Jack and Algy will follow them in. They both want a reconciliation, but agree to preserve a dignified silence if the two men do come in.

Jack and Algernon enter, whistling some dreadful popular tune from a British opera. The girls find that their vow of dignified silence is producing an unpleasant and distasteful effect, but Gwendolen asserts to Cecily that they will not be the first to speak – then immediately speaks, addressing Jack! Cecily, relieved, congratulates her on her invaluable common sense and immediately addresses a question to Algy: Why did he pretend to be her guardian's brother? In order that he might have an opportunity of meeting her, comes the reply. Gwendolen asks Jack if he pretended to have a brother in order to be able to come up to town to see her as often as possible. Yes, answers Jack. The girls find the answers satisfactory. The one remaining problem is the men's names, but Jack and Algy announce that they are both going to be rechristened Ernest that very afternoon. The road to matrimonial bliss is now open, and the two pairs embrace happily.

But all is not yet well. Merriman announces Lady Bracknell. She had followed Gwendolen after discovering her whereabouts by bribing her maid. Jack and Gwendolen declare that they are engaged to be married, but Lady Bracknell absolutely forbids the marriage. She then turns to Algernon and asks if this is the house in which his invalid friend Mr Bunbury resides. Algy stammeringly says no, then states that Bunbury is dead. He explains that the doctors found out that Bunbury could not live – so he died! Lady Bracknell says she is glad that Bunbury finally made up his mind to some definite course of action, and acted under proper medical advice! Algy then boldly declares that he is engaged to be married to Cecily Cardew.

The fact that Cecily is Jack's ward is enough to make Lady Bracknell behave coldly towards her. She turns to Jack and asks him if Miss Cardew is at all connected with any of the larger railway stations in London – a reference to Jack's origin that infuriates him. He coldly provides the name of Cecily's dead grandfather and his three addresses (the existence of three addresses inspires confidence in Lady Bracknell). He gives the name of Cecily's family solicitors, and irritably adds that he possesses certificates of Miss Cardew's birth, baptism, whooping cough, registration, vaccination, confirmation, and the measles; both the German and the English variety. So far Lady Bracknell is satisfied, but only mildly. She rises to go, but inquires first if Cecily has any little fortune. 'About £130,000 in the Funds', Jack replies airily, and bids her goodbye.

This new fact immediately transforms Lady Bracknell. Suddenly, she is totally in favour of the alliance, sits down again, and declares that Cecily possesses solid qualities. The dear child's hair can be improved by 'a thoroughly experienced French maid', and her profile has 'distinct social possibilities'. She declares that she does not approve of mercenary marriages, but gives her consent and advises Cecily and Algy to marry quickly, since long engagements 'give people the opportunity of finding out each other's character before marriage, which I think is never advisable'.

At this point Jack interrupts to inform Lady Bracknell that, as Miss Cardew's guardian, he considers her engagement to Algernon to be quite out of the question; Algy's moral character and untruthfulness make him an unfit husband for Cecily. Jack explains that Algy obtained admission to his house under the false pretence of being his brother; that he consumed an entire pint bottle of a wine Jack was especially reserving for himself; that he succeeded in the course of the afternoon in alienating Cecily's affections; that he devoured all the muffins; and that he was well aware all the time that Jack has no brother. Lady Bracknell finds no difficulty in forgiving Algernon, but Jack insists that his decision is unalterable.

Lady Bracknell turns to Cecily, discovers that the 'sweet child' is eighteen years old, and concludes that she will soon be of age and no longer in need of her guardian's consent to marry. Jack interrupts again and informs her that, according to the terms of her grandfather's will, Cecily does not come legally of age till she is thirty-five. This does not deter Lady Bracknell, who finds that thirty-five is a very attractive age. Besides, the money will have accumulated considerably by then! Algy is willing to wait seventeen years for Cecily, but she says that she couldn't possibly wait all that time. Lady Bracknell remarks that Cecily has a 'somewhat impatient nature' and appeals to Jack to reconsider his decision. The moment Lady Bracknell consents to his marriage with Gwendolen, Jack replies, he will most gladly allow her nephew to marry his ward. Lady Bracknell rises angrily, declares that what Jack proposes is out of the question, and prepares to depart with her daughter.

At this moment, Dr Chasuble enters and announces that everything is quite ready for the christenings. Lady Bracknell, desiring to know who is to be baptised, learns that it is Jack and Algy. She labels the idea 'grotesque and irreligious', and forbids Algy to waste his time and money in that way. Jack informs Dr Chasuble that the christenings are no longer 'of much practical value', a statement that grieves the Rector considerably, since it savours 'of the heretical views of the Anabaptists'. Since Jack's mood seems to be one peculiarly secular, Dr Chasuble decides to return to the church at once, where he says Miss Prism has been waiting for him for the last hour and a half.

'Miss Prism!' cries Lady Bracknell excitedly. Did she hear the Rector mention a Miss Prism? Yes! She has been Cecily's governess for the past three years, Jack says. Lady Bracknell demands to see her.

Suddenly, Miss Prism enters hurriedly, in search of Dr Chasuble. She catches sight of Lady Bracknell, grows pale, and looks anxiously round for an opportunity to escape. There is no escape, however. Lady Bracknell fixes her with a stony glare and bellows, 'Prism! Where is that baby?' The Canon starts back in horror. Jack and Algernon move to shield Gwendolen and Cecily from hearing the details of a scandal. Twenty-eight years ago, Lady Bracknell says, Miss Prism left Lord Bracknell's house with a perambulator that contained a male baby. She had never returned, and the police had found the perambulator a few weeks later containing only the manuscript of a three-volume novel 'of more than usually revolting sentimentality'. Trapped, Miss Prism is forced to admit that she had committed a terrible error that day, and had deposited the baby in a capacious handbag in which she had intended to place a novel she had written, and she had placed the novel in the perambulator. She admits she left the bag at Victoria Station, and sinks into a chair, quite crushed.

Jack becomes very excited and rushes from the room. A few moments later noises are heard overhead as if someone was throwing trunks about; then he returns with a handbag of black leather in his hand. 'Is this the handbag?' he asks Miss Prism. She examines it calmly and finds clear indications (an injury, a beverage stain, her initials) that it is indeed hers. She is delighted to have.it so unexpectedly restored to her, she declares. It has been a great inconvenience being without it all these years!

In a pathetic voice, Jack announces that more is restored to Miss Prism than the handbag, for he was the baby she placed in it. He embraces her and calls her mother, but she breaks away from him indignantly, declaring that she is unmarried. Jack assumes that he is her illegitimate child, and this makes her even more indignant. Turning to Lady Bracknell for an explanation, he is told that he is the son of her poor sister and consequently Algernon's elder brother.

'Was he christened?' asks Jack. Every luxury that money could buy, including christening, had been lavished on him by his fond and doting parents. What, then, is his first name? The same as his father's, the General. But what was General Moncrieff's first name? Lady Bracknell cannot remember! Neither can Algy, who says he was never on speaking terms with his father, since 'he died before I was a year old'. The Army Lists of the last 40 years are brought out, the General's name is found, and it turns out that his Christian names were – Ernest John! So Jack's name is really Ernest, after all, and he had been telling the truth to Gwendolen! Jack and Gwendolen embrace, and so do Algernon and Cecily. Even Dr Chasuble, a confirmed celibate, rejects his former views on marriage and embraces Miss Prism, who cries out enthusiastically: 'Frederick! At last!' The play ends with Jack declaring that he now realises 'the vital Importance of Being Earnest'.

NOTES AND GLOSSARY:

Anabaptists: a Christian sect that denied the validity of infant baptism and held that only adult baptism was valid. Dr Chasuble, however, accuses Jack of being an Anabaptist when Jack *rejects* adult baptism. This is an error on Wilde's part that he did not notice. Probably he had a mistaken notion about the basic doctrine of the Anabaptists. Another error in the play occurs in Act II, when Cecily tells Algy that they became engaged on the 14th of February and that they have been engaged for three months. This places the time of year as early May, whereas we are distinctly told at the beginning of Act II that the month is July. These errors are minor, however, and do not serve to detract from our enjoyment of the play

Part 3

Commentary

IT IS NOT POSSIBLE to understand *The Importance of Being Earnest* fully unless we see it as part of Oscar Wilde's total literary output. After he was seduced into homosexual practices by Robert Ross late in 1886, Wilde became very aware of the evil in himself and, by extension, in human nature. His ability to express the theme of evil in literature was also strengthened and sharpened, and he began to produce work after work dealing with evil, crime, and suffering. To simplify matters, we can divide Wilde's career from 1886 until he began writing *The Importance of Being Earnest* into three basic units:

(1) **The fairy tales.** Wilde first reacted to the evil in himself by writing a series of fairy tales. The fairy tale is a form of literature which introduces evil – witches, dragons, wicked giants, and so on – only to defeat it. The good and pure always triumph in those tales. Wilde's fairy tales deal for the most part not with external evil but with the evil in human nature, and are thus much more sophisticated than the usual such tale. The typical Wilde tale presents a hero who recognises the evil in himself but manages to crush and destroy it. Wilde said that these tales are for 'children from eight to eighty', which means that they are not only for children but also for adults who wish to remain in a childlike world of innocence. They are his attempt to fight the evil in himself and remain in the world of his two children, Cyril and Vyvyan. 'Lord Arthur Savile's Crime', 'The Selfish Giant', 'The Young King', and 'The Star-Child' are some of Wilde's best known fairy tales. He also wrote critical essays during this period, but the best of them – *The Decay of Lying* and *The Critic as Artist* – are written in a very playful style which, despite their seriousness, conveys the impression that the writer is a child at play.

(2) *The Picture of Dorian Gray.* By 1890, Wilde had come to the realisation that the evil in himself could not be controlled, and that he was becoming more and more involved homosexually. He therefore decided to explore the theme of human evil not within the harmless framework of the fairy tale but in a dark, sinister novel with a tragic ending. The result was *The Picture of Dorian Gray* (1890). As his name implies, the hero of this novel has a nature that is 'grey': he is neither all white nor all black. He begins in a state of childlike

innocence but is gradually corrupted. As the novel progresses, Dorian becomes more and more evil, and he finds beauty in evil, although he yearns at times for his lost innocence. Finally, he becomes so evil that he can no longer bear it. Discovering that he cannot recover his lost innocence, he grows desperate and accidentally kills himself. Despite the immoral behaviour of Dorian, the novel has a moral ending, for it shows what happens in the end to a person who cannot control his evil impulses. Nevertheless, *The Picture of Dorian Gray* was heavily attacked in the press for its immorality. Wilde's response was to repeat the theme of his novel in a play, *Lady Windermere's Fan*. In this play, Lady Windermere and Mrs Erlynne are presented as opposites. Lady Windermere considers herself to be entirely good, while Mrs Erlynne is considered by society to be completely bad. In the course of the action, both characters discover that their nature is grey, a mixture of good and evil. We also learn that Mrs Erlynne is Lady Windermere's supposedly dead mother. The two women, who at first appeared poles apart, turn out to be mother and daughter both in the flesh and in the spirit. The play, a light social comedy, proved very successful.

(3) *Salomé*. Wilde returned to the dark and sinister in a chilling one-act play, *Salomé*, which he wrote late in 1891. A symbolist play, *Salomé* is based on an episode in the Bible where Salomé, the daughter of Herodias, asks for, and receives, the head of John the Baptist. Salomé's behaviour has often been viewed as the ultimate in evil, for what can possibly be more terrible than requesting the head of a prophet? Wilde uses this tale to present a religion of Satan opposed to Christianity. In his play, the prophet Jokanaan (John the Baptist) is a man who has repressed his murderous sexual nature, while the cruel and lustful Salomé is presented as a symbol of human nature. In *Salomé*, human nature is not presented as 'grey' but as entirely black. Nor is Wilde unhappy about this. He declares that human nature is totally and irrevocably evil, then goes on to say that we should express the evil in ourselves instead of hiding it. Salomé and Jokanaan are portrayed as having an identical nature, but the difference is that Jokanaan hides his nature while Salomé expresses it fully. When *Salomé* was banned from the English stage by the Lord Chamberlain, Wilde once again responded by repeating the basic theme in a light social comedy. *A Woman of No Importance*, written in 1892, looks like a melodrama full of sparkling wit, but beneath its conventional surface is concealed the idea that human nature is totally evil. In these two plays, Oscar Wilde is a Satanist, preaching the acceptance and expression of inner depravity and denying that there is any goodness in human nature.

Like Dorian Gray, the protagonist of his novel, Oscar Wilde after his satanic plays felt that he had gone too far in the pursuit of evil beauty, and began to yearn for his lost innocence. The chief product of this reaction was *The Importance of Being Earnest,* which captures perfectly the world of childlike innocence; for the characters who inhabit the play are really babies who are playing at life. When Jack is making arrangements with Dr Chasuble to be christened, the Canon offers to christen him at five in the afternoon along with the newly-born Jenkins twins. Jack's response is this: 'Oh! I don't see much fun in being christened along with other babies. It would be childish.' In these lines, Jack refers to himself as a baby. And he is – a twenty-nine-year-old infant who never really grew up. The other characters in the play are also babies. Physically adult, they are mentally and psychologically still in the paradise of childhood, innocently and joyfully imitating the behaviour of real adults. When Jack and Algy are rejected by Gwendolen and Cecily towards the end of Act II, they begin by quarrelling, but the quarrel soon deteriorates into a fight over who is to eat the muffins the girls left behind. Jack snatches the muffin-dish from Algy, but Algy snatches it back and gobbles up the muffins. This is not the way adults behave; the fight over who is to eat the muffins is really a fight between two infants. Their attempt to marry is the attempt of two babies who have playfully decided to behave as people in the adult world do. Being infants, however, their behaviour naturally becomes quite babyish as soon as the game is temporarily interrupted. The entire play creates the impression of a group of children who have come together and decided to imitate the behaviour of people in the adult world. In *The Importance of Being Earnest,* Oscar Wilde – without going back to the fairy-tale genre – caught perfectly the world of childlike innocence, a world where no one can harm or be harmed.

The mood of innocence is captured not only by the action of the play but also – and more markedly – by the dialogue. For *The Importance of Being Earnest* is a nonsense play. It has frequently been called a comedy of manners, but perhaps it can hardly be placed in this category without some hesitation. The best examples of the comedy of manners (sometimes referred to as artificial comedy) are William Congreve's *The Way of the World* (1700) and Richard Brinsley Sheridan's *The School for Scandal* (1777). These plays present characters who behave immorally, but do so in such a gay, delightful way as to prevent the audience exercising moral judgement on them. Evil is present in the comedy of manners, but it is rendered harmless: we do not feel that it is real evil. *The Importance of Being Earnest* has those characteristics. However, one of the chief functions of the comedy of manners is to satirise the society of its time. *The*

Way of the World and *The School for Scandal* make great fun of the failings of the societies they portray. *The Importance of Being Earnest,* however, is not interested in satirising the upper-class English society of the end of the nineteenth century. Rather, it seeks to reduce this society to the level of childlike innocence in an attempt to escape from evil. Moreover, it does this mainly by presenting us with an essentially nonsensical dialogue. The dialogue in the typical comedy of manners is gay, witty, and hilarious, but it is not *nonsense.* Because the element of social satire is largely (but not entirely) missing, and because the dialogue is nonsensical, *The Importance of Being Earnest* cannot be firmly labelled a comedy of manners, although it does have many of the characteristics of this type of comedy.

It can more appropriately be categorised as a nonsense play. In the nineteenth century, a new literary form appeared in England known as nonsense writing. The chief examples of this form are Lewis Carroll's *Alice in Wonderland* (1865) and *Through the Looking Glass* (1872), and Edward Lear's *Book of Nonsense* (1846). When Alice meets Humpty Dumpty, for instance, she finds that when the huge egg speaks, he does not use words in their right meaning, and she dares to correct him. Humpty Dumpty replies indignantly that, when he uses a word, it means exactly what he wants it to mean, no more and no less. This is, of course, total nonsense, for if Humpty Dumpty attributes a private meaning to some of the words he uses, no one will be able to understand what he says. The farcical plays of W.S. Gilbert and the comic operas of Gilbert and Sullivan can also be said to belong to this new category of writing. Social satire is often one of the aims of nonsense literature, but it is not a necessary characteristic. Quite clearly, *The Importance of Being Earnest* is a nonsense play.

What can possibly be more nonsensical, for instance, than the following dialogue?

ALGERNON: (*retreating to back of sofa*) But why does she call herself little Cecily if she is your aunt and lives at Tunbridge Wells? (*Reading*) 'From little Cecily with her fondest love.'
JACK: (*moving to sofa and kneeling upon it*) My dear fellow, what on earth is there in that? Some aunts are tall, some aunts are not tall. That is a matter that surely an aunt may be allowed to decide for herself.

Or this:

ALGERNON: I am obliged to go up by the first train on Monday morning. I have a business appointment that I am anxious . . . to miss.
CECILY: Couldn't you miss it anywhere but in London?
ALGERNON: No: the appointment is in London.

Jack declares that a person surely should be allowed to decide for himself what his height ought to be – as though height were a matter of choice rather than heredity! Algy says he has to be in London on Monday afternoon because of a business appointment he wishes to miss – a totally absurd statement and the exact opposite of what a person would have normally said. By having his characters say the opposite of what is normal or expected, Wilde reduces the dialogue of his play to hilarious nonsense and introduces us into a paradise of innocence.

The Importance of Being Earnest is full of such nonsensical statements. 'I must say, Algernon', thunders Lady Bracknell, 'that I think it is high time that Mr Bunbury made up his mind whether he was going to live or to die. This shilly-shallying with the question is absurd. . . . I should be much obliged if you would ask Mr Bunbury, from me, to be kind enough not to have a relapse on Saturday, for I rely on you to arrange my music for me'. What is absurd about Lady Bracknell's statement, of course, is that she assumes Bunbury's health to be completely under his control! When Miss Prism says that she once wrote a novel, Cecily hopes it did not end happily, for happy endings 'depress me so much'. Miss Prism replies that 'the good ended happily, and the bad unhappily', and Cecily observes that 'it seems very unfair'. When Jack sadly announces the death of his brother to Miss Prism, she replies: 'What a lesson for him! I trust he will profit by it.' Algy at one point informs Cecily that they have to part. She responds as follows: 'It is always painful to part from people whom one has known for a very brief space of time. The absence of old friends one can endure with equanimity. But even a momentary separation from anyone to whom one has just been introduced is almost unbearable.' By turning everything upside down in the dialogue and standing reality on its head, Wilde creates a hilarious nonsensical world that returns us to the innocence of childhood.

Sometimes, the effect of nonsense in the dialogue is achieved in a manner slightly more subtle than simple inversion. When Jack explains to Lady Bracknell that he was found in a handbag at Victoria Station, he focuses time and again on unimportant details that create a nonsensical comic atmosphere. He explains, for instance, that he was named Worthing because the gentleman who found him happened to have a first-class ticket for Worthing in his pocket at the time. This is perfectly legitimate. The element of nonsense is introduced, however, when Jack continues the explanation by giving the geographical location of Worthing – it is in Sussex – and stating that it is a seaside resort. By mixing the important fact of how he got his name with completely irrelevant details about Worthing, Jack renders his total statement hilarious and nonsensical.

He then says he was found in a handbag, but goes on to describe it as 'a somewhat large, black leather handbag, with handles to it – an ordinary handbag in fact' – as though the physical appearance of the handbag is of great importance in his situation! He says that the handbag was in the cloakroom at Victoria Station – an important fact – but adds that it was the Brighton line, which merits a well-deserved response from Lady Bracknell: 'The line is immaterial, Mr Worthing.' This same method is used again at the end of the play, when Jack brings the handbag to Miss Prism. She identifies it as the same she lost many years ago, but – instead of inquiring about the fate of the baby she had placed in it – she moves to reclaim the bag. 'I am delighted to have it so unexpectedly restored to me', she says. 'It has been a great inconvenience being without it all these years.' Wherever one turns in the play, the dialogue is nonsensical.

We can sum up what happened in Wilde's career thus: after he wrote his satanic plays, he began to feel oppressed by an unbearable sense of evil and sin. He started to yearn for a return to innocence. The chief product of this reaction was *The Importance of Being Earnest*. In it, Wilde presented us with a group of adults who behave as children, and succeeded brilliantly in capturing a state of childlike innocence. To achieve this effect, he relied mainly on nonsensical dialogue. Thus, *The Importance of Being Earnest* is a play that takes us into a world of innocence and of nonsense. It is Wilde's assertion that a human being can remain as innocent as a child no matter how old he becomes.

However, there is more to *The Importance of Being Earnest* than that. For what is it, basically, that the play reduces to nonsense? An obvious answer is the upper-class English society that Wilde knew so well, the society that adopted him and turned him into a famous person. This is correct, but it is only part of the answer.

To answer the question completely, we must first go to Walter Pater's *The Renaissance* (1873) and remember that it remained Wilde's favourite book throughout most of his life. After his imprisonment, Wilde referred to *The Renaissance* (in *De Profundis*) as 'that book which had such a strange influence over my life'. In the famous conclusion to his book, Pater wrote that we can only receive unstable impressions of the outside world, and that

the whole scope of observation is dwarfed to the narrow chamber of the individual mind. Experience . . . is ringed round for each one of us by that thick wall of personality through which no real voice has ever pierced on its way to us, or from us to that which we can only conjecture to be without. Every one of those impressions is the impression of the individual in his isolation, each mind keeping as a solitary prisoner its own dream of a world.

In simple language, what Pater is saying is that the only thing we can really know is our own personality. Oscar Wilde accepted this view and wrote basically about himself. His dominant theme is the evil within himself, although he generalised from personal experience and spoke of the evil in human nature. It should come as no surprise, then, that what *The Importance of Being Earnest* reduces to nonsense is – Oscar Wilde! What Wilde does in the play is to take the basic themes and situations of his earlier literary works and present them to us again in an absurd, farcical manner, thus unmasking them as nonsense. The message of *The Importance of Being Earnest* is that Wilde's earlier works are nonsensical, and that he lives in a childlike world of innocence where evil is a silly, harmless thing. *The Importance of Being Earnest* earnestly reveals to us Wilde's real world, his true personality, as he saw it at that time.

Before continuing the discussion, it is necessary to give a brief summary of the major works that Wilde treats farcically in *The Importance of Being Earnest*.

'Lord Arthur Savile's Crime'

This is Wilde's first fairy tale, written in a delightful, witty style beneath which there is a good deal of intellectual content. The hero of the tale, Lord Arthur Savile, is a young, handsome aristocrat. We first meet him at a very expensive party, and are told about him that, until that night, 'he had lived the delicate and luxurious life of a young man of birth and fortune, a life exquisite in its freedom from sordid care, its beautiful boyish insouciance'. In other words, he has spent his life so far in a paradise of childlike innocence. This happy state cannot last, though, for people grow up. Arthur is now a grown man and is engaged to be married to a beautiful girl called Sibyl.

At the party, he meets Podgers, a palmist, who can predict the future of any person by examining his hand. Podgers reads Lord Arthur's hand and grows frightened. Pressed to reveal what he has seen, the fat and sweaty Podgers predicts that Arthur is destined to commit murder. He conceals from the young man, though, that it is he – Podgers – whom Arthur will murder.

Podgers's prediction changes Lord Arthur's life in a flash, for it brings him suddenly face-to-face with an evil streak within himself. He dashes out into the cold night, his hands and forehead on fire, and wanders 'into narrow, shameful alleys' full of prostitutes, violence, and poverty. He escapes from this dark underworld at daybreak, returns home, and goes to sleep. When he wakes, he finds himself in a sparkling world, more beautiful than the one from which he had fallen – 'Never had life seemed lovelier to him, never had the things of evil seemed more remote'. He goes into his luxurious bathroom and steps into the water in the marble tank. 'He plunged hastily in, till the cool ripples touched throat and hair, and then dipped his head right under, as though he would have wiped away the stain of some shameful memory.' Symbolically, this is an adult baptism. After experiencing evil, Arthur cleanses his soul and is born anew; his bathtub christening initiates him into this new world, much as a baptised infant is born again in Christ after having been born in original sin.

But this is not the end of Arthur's ordeal. His fiancée, the beautiful Sibyl, is an embodiment of total perfection and purity. Sibyl 'was to him a symbol of all that is good and noble', we are told. He cannot marry her until he has himself become totally pure, and he has still not committed murder. So Arthur sets out to commit murder before marrying Sibyl, thereby fulfilling Podgers's prediction and getting it out of the way.

He decides to murder the harmless Lady Clementina, and sends her a poisoned pill. She dies a natural death, however, without taking the pill. Arthur at first thinks he has succeeded, but is shocked and dismayed when he learns her death was natural. He then decides to murder the Dean of Chichester and sends him a bomb in a clock, but again he fails. He then sinks into despair, decides not to make any more murder attempts, and walks dejectedly to the Thames Embankment, where he sits till well past midnight. When he rises to leave, he runs across Podgers and quickly flings him into the river! After successfully committing murder, he marries Sibyl and they live happily for ever after.

The student should consider the following points about this tale:

(1) Podgers, although he has an existence separate from Arthur's, is presented as part of Arthur's personality, an evil and corrupt part. Thus, Arthur does not become completely pure until he has killed Podgers. The murder, paradoxically, is a form of self-purification, but it is nonetheless a crime, for a human being is killed.

(2) Wilde presents the future as completely predetermined. Arthur in the tale is predestined to commit murder. The person he is to kill and the time of the murder are also predetermined, and nothing he can do can change this.

(3) Arthur begins in a world of childlike innocence, but when he reaches maturity, this world is destroyed. He is forced to confront the evil in himself and in the outside world. He destroys this evil, however, and enters a new world of innocence superior to the one he lost.

(4) After Arthur is plunged into the evil world of Podgers, he escapes from it, cleanses his soul, then symbolically re-christens himself in his bathtub.

(5) Sibyl is presented as a perfect and totally pure girl.

'The Soul of Man under Socialism'

In this essay, written around 1890, Wilde stated that the human soul can achieve total freedom only if the class system is abolished. He argued against the ownership of private property, taking refuge nervously in wit:

> Property not only has duties, but has so many duties that its possession to any large extent is a bore. It involves endless claims upon one, endless attention to business, endless bother. If property had simply pleasures we could stand it; but its duties make it unbearable. In the interests of the rich we must get rid of it.

Wilde also said in this essay that the existence of the poor poisons the lives of the rich and gives them a guilty conscience.

The Picture of Dorian Gray

The novel begins with Dorian Gray, a very handsome young man, having his picture painted by Basil Hallward. Dorian is still in a state of innocence. However, he is subjected to a demonic sermon by Lord Henry Wotton, in which Lord Henry preaches to him that he should live a complete life devoted to the pursuit of sensations: 'Live! Live the wonderful life that is in you! Let nothing be lost upon you. Be always searching for new sensations.'

Lord Henry's sermon has a corrupting influence on Dorian, and when the youth sees his completed picture, he wishes that he could remain eternally young while the picture grows old instead. He then accepts Lord Henry as his guide and tutor in life. Dorian's descent into evil is a gradual process, however. He falls in love with a very innocent and immature young actress, Sibyl Vane, in his attempt to satisfy a new 'passion for sensations'. But he soon rejects her, and she commits suicide. After Sibyl's suicide, Dorian's picture changes, acquiring a touch of cruelty. With a shock, Dorian remembers the wish he made in Basil Hallward's studio and realises that it has been granted. He removes his picture and locks it up in the attic of his home.

Bit by bit, Dorian begins to pursue a double life. He presents a moral face to respectable society, but also pursues a secret life of sin.

As he becomes more and more involved in sin and evil, his picture reflects the corruption of his soul while he himself remains young and innocent-looking. Often, he would go to the attic, unveil the picture, and look at it: 'He would examine with minute care, and sometimes with a monstrous and terrible delight, the hideous lines that seared the wrinkling forehead or crawled around the heavy sensual mouth, wondering sometimes which were the more horrible, the signs of sin or the signs of age.'

Dorian lives like this for twenty years, but finally goes too far: he murders Basil Hallward. The murder creates a feeling of revulsion in him and he tries to retrace his steps and recapture his lost innocence. He fails, and finally, in despair, he stabs his picture, identifying it with his conscience. The result is that Dorian the man ages suddenly and dies, while the picture regains its initial appearance of youth and innocence. Dorian's servants find him dead in the attic, old and sin-scarred, with a knife in his heart.

The basic points to remember about *The Picture of Dorian Gray* are the following:

(1) Throughout most of the novel, Dorian leads a double life. He presents a respectable face to society, but his moral personality is a mask. Every now and then, he disappears for a lengthy period of time. During his mysterious disappearances, he leads a life of evil and sinful pleasure. Although people begin to suspect more and more that the real Dorian is an evil man, he is never discovered in his lifetime. Discovery would have meant his social ruin.

(2) Lord Henry Wotton is presented as a Satan-figure in the novel. He is not, of course, the real Satan, but he does function as Dorian's private Devil, leading him into sin and corruption.

(3) Dorian is delineated as predetermined by his character to pursue a life of sin. Again, therefore, we have the theme of predestination.

Salomé

This is Wilde's most terrifying and evil play. It is also a highly symbolic and complex work. The setting is a feast and the time is the period of the coming of Jesus Christ. As the Tetrarch Herod and his sinful wife Herodias eat and drink with their many guests, Herod begins to lust after his wife's daughter, Princess Salomé. Salomé breaks away from the feast and goes out into the pure night air. There she hears the voice of Jokanaan (John the Baptist) predicting the coming of Christ. Jokanaan is imprisoned in a dark underground cistern. Salomé orders the Captain of the Guard, a young Syrian, to release the prophet and bring him to her. At first, the young Syrian refuses because the Tetrarch has absolutely forbidden such a thing. The princess, however, uses her sexual charms on the Syrian captain, and he releases Jokanaan.

Princess Salomé finds the prophet very attractive sexually and begins to woo him. Jokanaan, however, calls her a daughter of adultery, rejects her, and returns voluntarily to his prison. Rejected, she becomes intent on destroying the prophet. The young Syrian, realising that Salomé loves Jokanaan and not him, kills himself.

Herod emerges from his palace. He continues to woo Salomé and offers her the throne of her mother if she will dance for him. Salomé refuses at first, then agrees to dance after Herod promises to grant her any request she makes. She dances the dance of the seven veils, then asks for the head of Jokanaan as her reward. Herod is shocked and tries to dissuade her, but she insists and he finally yields.

Jokanaan is beheaded, and the severed head is brought to Salomé, who proceeds to 'feast' on it, biting and kissing it and comparing it to a ripe fruit. Even the lustful and evil Herod is horrified by this. He orders Salomé to be killed, and his soldiers crush her with their shields.

In this play, Wilde presents Salomé as a symbol of human nature. Her cruelty and sexual perversity are common to all people, Wilde feels. Jokanaan is also murderous and lustful in the play, but he has repressed his personality. Through the symbolism, the prophet is shown as also lusting for Salomé. His words continually betray his lust through their double meaning.

The main points to keep in mind about *Salomé* are the following:

(1) Salomé rejects Herod's banquet because she wants a sexual feast. She wants to feast on Jokanaan's body, and when she finds that she cannot obtain the prophet alive, she kills him and 'feasts' on his severed head.

(2) Jokanaan too is lustful, but he has hidden his lust even from himself. The words he utters, however, often have a double meaning that show him to be strongly attracted to Salomé despite his rejection of her.

An Ideal Husband

This play, a social comedy, was written shortly before *The Importance of Being Earnest*. For our purposes, there is only one scene in it that is important. Mrs Cheveley, the villainess of the play, tries to blackmail Sir Robert Chiltern, an honest politician who committed only one serious error in his past. Lord Goring, Sir Robert's friend, finds a snake-bracelet which Mrs Cheveley had earlier lost, and recognises it as having been stolen by her. When she tries to reclaim the bracelet, he corners her and exposes her as a thief. In this way, Lord Goring vanquishes her and saves his friend.

Now that a summary of the main works that *The Importance of Being Earnest* reduces to nonsense has been given, it is possible to look at the characters of *Earnest* more closely.

Jack

At the age of twenty-nine, Jack is still a child who plays the game of being adult. Throughout the play, we feel that he is an infant of about five years who has agreed with a group of other infants to imitate playfully the behaviour of the adults he sees around him every day. When Dr Chasuble offers to christen him with the newly-born Jenkins twins, Jack replies that he doesn't see 'much fun in being christened along with other babies', thereby referring to himself as a baby and also indicating that he regards his behaviour as 'fun'. He exists in a carefree world of childlike innocence where evil is a totally harmless, silly thing, and where no one can really hurt anyone or come to any harm.

This mood of innocence is strengthened greatly by the non-sensical dialogue that is uttered by the characters in the play. Some of the nonsense is uttered by Jack, although he is more usually the listener as his friend Algernon makes one nonsensical statement after another. 'Oh, that's nonsense, Algy', he cries at one point. 'You never talk anything but nonsense.'

As a character, his basic situation reduces to nonsense the very serious and dangerous double life that Dorian Gray led. Like Dorian, Jack has two identities. In the country, he is the respectable Mr Jack Worthing, the guardian of Cecily Cardew, and is therefore forced to adopt a very high moral tone on all subjects. Cecily observes that her Uncle Jack is so serious that she thinks he cannot be quite well, while the morally pompous Miss Prism says that Jack's 'gravity of demeanour is especially to be recommended in one so comparatively young as he is. I know no one who has a higher sense of duty and responsibility'. This identity is a mask, however. Jack's real personality emerges when he goes to London on pleasure trips. He has invented a fictitious wicked younger brother called Ernest who lives in London and gets into all sorts of trouble, and he uses this excuse to disappear from the country whenever he wishes. In London, however, he himself assumes the name of Ernest and lives entirely for pleasure. His real personality, like Dorian, is the wicked one. Wickedness, however, is a totally harmless, innocent thing in this play.

Had Dorian been exposed in his lifetime, he would have been rejected by society and disgraced forever. Jack *is* exposed in the play: everyone discovers that he has been leading a double life. Far from being disgraced, however, he is quickly forgiven by Gwendolen and the others. Jack's double identity is a reduction to nonsense of the double life that Dorian Gray led, for it reduces Dorian's situation to the level of innocence and playfulness.

In 'Lord Arthur Savile's Crime', Arthur had been spiritually reborn after facing and defeating an evil streak in himself, and had put the seal on his rebirth by christening himself in his bathtub. Jack's attempts to baptise himself reduce to absurdity the situation of Lord Arthur. Jack wishes to be christened for the nonsensical reason that he wants to change his name to Ernest, since Gwendolen will not marry him otherwise. The entire idea of spiritual rebirth is treated playfully and rendered absurd here. In the paradise of innocence that Jack inhabits, there is no need for any spiritual development whatsoever. There is no need for him to purge himself of evil because evil is not a real thing.

Finally, Lord Arthur had to commit a crime before he could marry Sibyl. Jack also finds himself forced to murder someone as a prelude to marriage. 'If Gwendolen accepts me', he says, 'I am going to kill my brother, indeed I think I'll kill him in any case.' Arthur's murder of Podgers was a real crime, despite Podgers's symbolic status, while Jack's brother is a fictitious creature, entirely a figment of Jack's imagination. The 'murder' that Jack commits, then, is totally harmless and a parody of Arthur's crime. It may also be considered a reduction to harmlessness and nonsense of Dorian Gray's murder of Basil Hallward.

Algernon

Like Jack, Algernon gives us the impression of being an infant pretending to be an adult. He lives in a carefree world of innocence where he gobbles up the cucumber sandwiches he ordered for his aunt, fights over a muffin-dish with Jack immediately after Cecily has deserted him, and in general regards the entire world as a playpen built especially for him.

To a large extent, the atmosphere of nonsense in the play is generated by Algy's many absurd utterances. At one point, he says: 'I hate people who are not serious about meals. It is so shallow of them.' Another nonsensical statement he makes is the following: 'It is awfully hard work doing nothing. However, I don't mind hard work where there is no definite object of any kind.' When Cecily asks him if his hair curls naturally, he replies: 'Yes, darling, with a little help from others.' Jack at one point says that it is none of Algy's business whether Jack and Gwendolen are likely to get married or not. Algy replies: 'If it was my business, I wouldn't talk about it. . . . It is very vulgar to talk about one's own business. Only people like stockbrokers do that, and then merely at dinner parties.'

Like Jack, Algy leads a double life. In London, he is under the constant supervision of his aunt, Lady Bracknell, and therefore has to behave properly and dine with such respectable people as Mary Farquhar, who constantly flirts with her own husband! He has invented an invalid friend who lives in the country, however, and whenever he wishes to disappear for a period in pursuit of pleasure, he pretends that Bunbury is quite ill and that he must go to him. As in Jack's case, Algy's double life is a reduction to absurdity of Dorian Gray's situation. His desire to be christened mocks Lord Arthur's baptism, and his 'killing' of Bunbury parodies Arthur's murder of Podgers and Dorian's killing of Basil. It is no accident that he and Jack turn out to be brothers in the end, for the two are brothers in personality.

Algy's tremendous appetite – he is always hungry and constantly eating throughout the play – reduces to innocence and nonsense the sin-tainted feast of *Salomé*. The earlier feast culminated in Salomé 'feasting' on the severed head of a prophet. Algy's appetite, however, does not lead him to do anything naughtier than eating Lady Bracknell's cucumber sandwiches and Jack's muffins. Unlike Salomé's blood-thirsty sexual appetite, Algy's is delightfully funny and harmless.

The scene where Algy finds Jack's cigarette case and discovers that Jack leads a double life renders absurd a similar scene in *An Ideal Husband*. In the earlier play, Lord Goring found Mrs Cheveley's snake-bracelet. When she attempted to get it back, she was exposed as a thief and defeated. In *The Importance of Being Earnest*, the exposure of Jack is shrouded in an atmosphere of childlike innocence. Nor does the exposure harm Jack's social position or his chances of marrying Gwendolen. Quite the contrary, it deepens his friendship with Algy, a fellow 'Bunburyist'.

Gwendolen

Another grown-up baby, she gives the impression of living in a world of childlike innocence despite the fact that she is a highly attractive young lady whose chief concern in the play is to marry Jack. In 'Lord Arthur Savile's Crime', marriage represented the dividing line between innocence and the adult world, but in *The Importance of Being Earnest* it is simply part of the never-ending game of innocence and nonsense. Despite her engagement to Jack, Gwendolen remains an innocent from beginning to end.

In Act I, she overwhelms Jack with a barrage of witty nonsense. When he declares that he has an intense admiration for her, she replies: 'Yes, I am quite aware of the fact. And I often wish that in public, at any rate, you had been more demonstrative.' A bit later, she says: 'We live, as I hope you know, Mr Worthing, in an age of ideals. The fact is constantly mentioned in the more expensive monthly magazines, and has reached the provincial pulpits I am told.' When Jack goes on his knees and formally asks her to marry him, she replies: 'Of course I will, darling. How long you have been about it! I am afraid you have had very little experience in how to propose.' Her most nonsensical statement, however, comes when she declares that her ideal has always been to love someone named Ernest, that the name Ernest is the most attractive thing about Jack, and that she couldn't possibly marry him if his name were not Ernest. In Act II, however, she meets her match in Cecily. After the two girls discover that they are both engaged to Mr Ernest Worthing, they have a verbal duel in which Cecily clearly emerges as the wittier of the two.

Gwendolen in the play is meant as a reduction to absurdity of the Sibyl of 'Lord Arthur Savile's Crime'. In that fairy tale, Sibyl was presented as a pure and perfect woman who required an equally perfect and pure husband. When Jack informs Gwendolen that he considers her to be 'quite perfect', however, she immediately reduces the idea to nonsense: 'Oh! I hope I am not that. It would leave no room for developments, and I intend to develop in many directions.' And indeed, her vanity – she loves to be admired – and her total frankness about it, though wrapped in an atmosphere of absurdity, show that she is not perfect. The ill temper she displays in Act II during her clash with Cecily further illustrates her lack of perfection. Moreover, she ends up marrying a 'wicked' man. She discovers that Jack leads a double life, that he is a liar, and that his many trips to London were for the sake of pleasure. When she asks him why he pretended to have a brother, she adds another question that really provides Jack with the answer he is expected to give: 'Was it in order that you might have an opportunity of coming up to town to see me as often as possible?' When Jack says yes, Gwendolen states: 'I have the gravest doubts upon the subject. But I intend to crush them. This is not the moment for German scepticism.' Despite the fact that Jack is a liar and a pleasure-seeker, he is not asked to purify himself. It is his name that forms an obstacle to marriage, and when he announces that he is going to be rechristened Ernest, Gwendolen embraces him in delight. The situation is totally absurd.

Cecily

At the age of eighteen Cecily, like Gwendolen, is an innocent. Lady Bracknell and the others call her a child, and she is indeed a child in her playful, irresponsible attitude towards life as is evident from her first appearance as the pupil of Miss Prism.

Her conversation is a steady stream of witty, nonsensical utterances. In fact, she is the wittiest person in the play, and is the only one who is able to defeat Algernon at his own game of making nonsensical statements. When Miss Prism calls her to her German lesson, Cecily complains that German 'isn't at all a becoming language. I know perfectly well that I look quite plain after my German lesson'. Algy, masquerading as Ernest, says that he is going to reform then declares that he is hungry, and Cecily replies: 'How thoughtless of me. I should have remembered that when one is going to lead an entirely new life, one requires regular and wholesome meals.' When Algy starts paying her extravagant compliments, she opens her diary and starts writing them down. Taken by surprise, Algy coughs, and Cecily says: 'Oh, don't cough, Ernest. When one is dictating one should speak fluently and not cough. Besides, I don't know how to spell a cough.' The most nonsensical thing about Cecily, however, is that she refuses to marry a man whose name is not Ernest.

Like Gwendolen, Cecily is a reduction to absurdity of Sibyl in 'Lord Arthur Savile's Crime'. Algernon says to her: 'I hope, Cecily, I shall not offend you if I state quite frankly and openly that you seem to me to be in every way the visible personification of absolute perfection.' She is delighted to hear this, and dashes off to write it down in her diary, thereby revealing how vain she really is. She prays Algy not to stop, but to continue making compliments that she can record in her diary! Like Gwendolen, she discovers that her fiancé is a liar and 'wicked', but very quickly forgives him, insisting only that his name should be Ernest. It is no accident that Cecily and Gwendolen team up in the end and agree to call one another 'sister', for they are very much alike in personality.

In 'Lord Arthur Savile's Crime' and *The Picture of Dorian Gray,* Wilde presented his characters as predetermined. Lord Arthur especially, in the former tale, has no free will whatsoever. This idea is dissolved into hilarious nonsense in the scene where Algy proposes to Cecily only to discover that he has already been engaged to her for three whole months. His engagement to Cecily being predetermined, it occurred before he met her!

ALGERNON: Darling! And when was the engagement actually settled?

CECILY: On the 14th of February last. Worn out by your entire ignorance of my existence, I determined to end the matter one way or the other, and after a long struggle with myself I accepted you under this dear old tree here. The next day I bought this little ring in your name, and this is the little bangle with the true lovers' knot I promised you always to wear.
ALGERNON: Did I give you this? It's very pretty, isn't it?
CECILY: Yes, you've wonderfully good taste, Ernest.

Reading this, we get the impression of a clairvoyant revealing a person's future to him – with the exception that, in Algy's case, the future has already occurred.

Finally, Oscar Wilde always wrote about himself in his works. Since he believed, like Walter Pater, that the only thing a person can really know is his own personality, he always began by exploring his inner self, then expressed this self in his writings. Great fun is made of this when Cecily says to Algy of her diary: 'It is simply a very young girl's record of her own thoughts and impressions, and consequently meant for publication. When it appears in volume form I hope you will order a copy.'

Lady Bracknell

Lady Bracknell is the perfect embodiment of the attitudes and rules of conduct of the British aristocracy. Snobbish and superior in her behaviour, she is mainly interested in finding a suitable husband for Gwendolen, her only daughter, although she also seeks to dominate her nephew, Algernon. Throughout, however, the impression she creates is that of a child pretending to be an elderly British aristocrat – a child who has learned extremely well the rules of the game she is playing and refuses to make a single mistake.

The atmosphere of childlike innocence generated by Lady Bracknell is the result not only of her hilariously pompous behaviour but also of the many witty, nonsensical statements she makes. We first meet her when she arrives at Algernon's flat. She apologises for being late, saying: 'I am sorry if we are a little late, Algernon, but I was obliged to call on dear Lady Harbury. I hadn't been there since her poor husband's death. I never saw a woman so altered; she looks quite twenty years younger.' Learning of Bunbury's 'death' in Act III, she says: 'I am glad . . . that he made up his mind at the last to some definite course of action, and acted under proper medical advice.' On hearing the name of Miss Prism towards the end of the play, she inquires if this Miss Prism is 'a female of repellent aspect, remotely connected with education'. Dr Chasuble's indignant reply is that 'she is the most cultivated of ladies, and the very picture of respectability'. Lady Bracknell quickly retorts that 'it is obviously the same person'.

In her militant dislike of private property, Lady Bracknell reduces to nonsense the views advanced by Wilde in *The Soul of Man Under Socialism*. While she is interviewing Jack in Act I, she asks him what his income is:

> JACK: Between seven and eight thousand a year.
> LADY BRACKNELL: (*makes a note in her book*) In land, or in investments?
> JACK: In investments, chiefly.
> LADY BRACKNELL: That is satisfactory. What between the duties expected of one during one's lifetime, and the duties exacted from one after one's death, land has ceased to be either a profit or a pleasure. It gives one position, and prevents one from keeping it up. That's all that can be said about land.

Lady Bracknell is as opposed to the ownership of large stretches of private property as the most ardent socialist, but this does not mean that she is against the class system. Quite the contrary, she is very devoted to preserving the privileges enjoyed by the upper-classes and rejects Jack because of his possible lower-class origins without feeling any pangs of conscience. In advocating socialism, Wilde had argued that the possession of property 'to any large extent . . . involves . . . endless attention to business, endless bother. . . . In the interests of the rich we must get rid of it'. Lady Bracknell agrees that private property is a bother but finds a solution to the problem other than socialism: she insists that the rich should invest their money rather than place it in land! Cecily is all the more attractive because her £130,000 are 'in the Funds', not in land.

In her attempts to keep Jack and Gwendolen apart, Lady Bracknell is destroying their chances of happiness and is therefore monstrous in her behaviour. This is a parody of Lord Henry Wotton in *The Picture of Dorian Gray*. In that novel, Lord Henry functioned as Dorian's private Satan, leading him ultimately to death and destruction. Jack says of Lady Bracknell at one point: 'Never met such a Gorgon . . . I don't really know what a Gorgon is like, but I am quite sure that Lady Bracknell is one. In any case, she is a monster, without being a myth, which is rather unfair.' But Lady Bracknell, unlike Lord Henry, is a harmless monster. In the world of *The Importance of Being Earnest*, an unhappy ending is quite out of the question, so Jack is discovered in the end to be Lady Bracknell's nephew and is allowed to marry Gwendolen. Lady Bracknell emerges as a harmless, nonsensical Gorgon.

Dr Chasuble

Dr Chasuble is a reduction to absurdity of John the Baptist as Wilde presented him in *Salomé*. Like Jokanaan (John the Baptist), Dr Chasuble is continually christening people. When Jack asks him in Act II if he knows how to christen, the Canon looks astounded but Miss Prism replies for him: 'It is, I regret to say, one of the Rector's most constant duties in this parish. I have often spoken to the poorer classes on the subject. But they don't seem to know what thrift is.'

Jokanaan had a hidden lust for the beautiful Salomé, but he repressed it and denied its existence even to himself. Throughout *Salomé*, however, the prophet makes statements which have a double meaning. The unintended meaning betrays his repressed sexual impulses. In *The Importance of Being Earnest*, Dr Chasuble follows the teachings and practice of the Primitive Church as regards sex and marriage. Since the Primitive Church did not allow its clergy to marry or have any form of sexual intercourse, he rejects the idea of marriage and remains celibate. However, he entertains a lust for Miss Prism, who is middle-aged and unattractive. His attempt to hide this lust results in several hilarious slips of the tongue.

Even Dr Chasuble's name has a double meaning. A chasuble (pronounced *chaz-uble*) is an ecclesiastical vestment worn by the celebrant at Mass. The name can be pronounced in another way, however (*chase-able*), which would suggest that the Rector is capable of being chased very successfully by women. And indeed, Miss Prism does chase after him in the play and succeeds in netting him. When Dr Chasuble visits the Manor House and finds Miss Prism teaching Cecily, he observes that, were he fortunate enough to be Miss Prism's pupil, he 'would hang upon her lips'. What he means, of course, is that he would be very attentive, but the phrase can also be understood sexually. Dr Chasuble, embarrassed, apologises and explains that he was simply using a metaphor drawn from bees. A few lines later, however, he refers to Miss Prism as Egeria – a classical allusion, he explains. But Egeria was a beautiful nymph who was both the teacher and lover of King Numa Pompilius – thus another slip of the tongue.

Jokanaan was beheaded at the end of *Salomé*, but Dr Chasuble simply admits to himself that he is attracted to Miss Prism and embraces her. His situation reduces that of Jokanaan to harmlessness and nonsense.

Miss Prism

Miss Prism is the embodiment of the Victorian middle-class code of morality and duty. A stiff and intellectual person, she expects Cecily to behave seriously and study hard, and she strongly disapproves of the immoral character of Jack's fictitious brother Ernest.

In the realm of literature, Miss Prism insists that fiction should preach morality – an attitude that especially irritated Wilde. (*The Picture of Dorian Gray* was heavily attacked because it was considered immoral, and *Salomé* was banned from the English stage.) Miss Prism declares that she once wrote a three-volume novel, and that in it 'the good ended happily, and the bad unhappily. That is what Fiction means.' Hilariously, though, she became so preoccupied with the manuscript of her novel that she lost a baby she had been entrusted with – an unforgivable breach of duty after which she disappeared. She is not exposed until the end of the play.

Another breach of duty comes when she leaves Cecily to study alone, and goes for a walk with Dr Chasuble. She is deeply attracted to the Rector but, unlike Gwendolen and Cecily, she hides her sexual feelings. She proposes marriage to Dr Chasuble in a very oblique and roundabout manner, suggesting that it is his moral duty to get married, since a bachelor turns himself into a permanent public temptation. Her attempt to hide her feelings, however, leads her to make slips of the tongue very similar to Dr Chasuble's. She suggests a mature woman for the Rector, and says: 'Maturity can always be depended on. Ripeness can be trusted. Young women are green.' What she means is intellectual ripeness, but her words have a double meaning and can also be understood as referring to sexual ripeness. Dr Chasuble understands them sexually, and Miss Prism quickly explains that she was using a metaphor drawn from fruits. To a large extent, she is the female counterpart of the Rector.

To envelop her in childlike innocence, Wilde gives her several nonsensical lines. When she leaves Cecily to study alone, she asks her to read Political Economy but adds: 'The chapter on the Fall of the Rupee you may omit. Even these metallic problems have their melodramatic side.' (The rupee is the basic monetary unit in India.) When Jack announces the death of his brother Ernest, she says: 'What a lesson for him! I trust he will profit by it.'

Despite Miss Prism's exposure at the end of the play, all ends happily for her: she marries the man of her choice.

The minor characters

Lane. He is Algernon's manservant, who also leaves us with the impression of being a child who is pretending to be an adult. His relationship with his employer is a perfectly happy and harmonious one – a refutation of Wilde's view, in 'The Soul of Man Under Socialism', that the class system poisons the lives of the rich and makes the poor unhappy. Lane and Algy seem instinctively to understand one another. When Algy consumes all the cucumber sandwiches meant for Lady Bracknell, Lane covers up for him without any prior instructions. The lines uttered by Lane are mainly nonsensical. He says, for instance: 'I have had very little experience of [marriage] myself up to the present. I have only been married once. That was in consequence of a misunderstanding between myself and a young person.'

Merriman. He is Jack's butler, and he appears only to announce the arrival of someone, to inform Algernon that the dogcart is waiting for him, or to lay tea for Cecily and Gwendolen. Like Lane, however, he is loyal to his employer, and warns him by coughing when Lady Bracknell arrives in Act III while the two pairs of lovers are clasped in an embrace.

Balanced and opposed characters

Wilde seems to present us with pairs of characters in *The Importance of Being Earnest*. Thus, Jack and Algernon share certain basic character-istics of personality and turn out to be brothers at the end of the play. Cecily and Gwendolen are alike in many respects; they team up towards the end of Act II and start calling each other sister. Miss Prism and Dr Chasuble are both serious, sexually shy, and guardians of the moral code, and they marry in the end. Only Lady Bracknell is left without a counterpart in the play.

Wilde also uses counterpoint to strengthen the identification of his characters. Miss Prism and Dr Chasuble stand opposed to Jack, Algernon, Cecily, and Gwendolen. The opposition is between serious-ness and gaiety, moral duty and irresponsible pleasure-seeking. By placing these two sets of characters in contrast, Wilde sharpens the impression they make upon us.

Part 4

Hints for study

Points for detailed study

The great problem that faces any student of *The Importance of Being Earnest* is that the play appears at first to be meaningless: there is nothing to say about it. The temptation is simply to summarise its plot and feel that you have discussed the play. Simple plot summary – retelling the story in your own words – must be avoided at all costs. You should retell a part of the story only when it supports an idea that you are trying to prove.

In discussing *The Importance of Being Earnest*, you should remember that there are three major ideas. These are best approached in the following order:

(1) *The Importance of Being Earnest* is a play of innocence. This is the easiest idea and one that you should stress when you write about the play. As was explained in Part 3, Oscar Wilde in this play tries to escape from evil by creating a world of childlike innocence where everything is treated playfully and no one can come to harm. To discuss this theme effectively, you should know something about Wilde's earlier works, especially *The Picture of Dorian Gray* and *Salomé*. A brief summary of these two works is provided in Part 3.

(2) *The Importance of Being Earnest* is a nonsense play. This idea is connected to the first one. To create an atmosphere of innocence, Wilde resorts to the device of nonsense. The dialogue of the play, for instance, is often pure nonsense, and it would be a good idea to memorise two or three brief nonsensical statements and to quote them in your examination. The behaviour of the characters in the play is also often nonsensical. A good example is the fight that Jack and Algy have over a muffin-dish at the end of Act II.

(3) *The Importance of Being Earnest* is a reduction to nonsense of Wilde's earlier works. This is the most difficult theme with which you will have to deal. You cannot write about it unless you know something about Wilde's earlier writings. A short summary of the relevant works is given in Part 3 and this emphasises the main points you should know. If you study these summaries well, then read the analysis of the characters in *The Importance of Being Earnest*, and you should be able

to write intelligently and at great length about the play. Always remember that this third idea is an expansion of the idea that *The Importance of Being Earnest* is a nonsense play.

You may also be asked to write about the structure of *The Importance of Being Earnest*. In this case, the sample answer given later in this Part should prove valuable to you, for it explains the principles on which Wilde drew the characters of his play.

Central quotations

The quotations given below are all central. (*i*) Read them carefully. (*ii*) Analyse each quotation, explaining why it is central. (*iii*) Relate the quotation to an important idea in the play other than the one you have already discussed. This test will allow you to determine to what extent you have understood the main ideas, themes and purpose of the play.

(1) JACK: My dear Algy, I don't know whether you will be able to understand my real motives. You are hardly serious enough. When one is placed in the position of guardian, one has to adopt a very high moral tone on all subjects. It's one's duty to do so. And as a high moral tone can hardly be said to conduce very much to either one's health or one's happiness, in order to get up to town I have always pretended to have a younger brother by the name of Ernest, who lives in the Albany, and gets into the most dreadful scrapes. That, my dear Algy, is the whole truth pure and simple.

(2) JACK: You're quite perfect, Miss Fairfax.
GWENDOLEN: Oh! I hope I am not that. It would leave no room for developments, and I intend to develop in many directions.

(3) LADY BRACKNELL: What between the duties expected of one during one's lifetime, and the duties exacted from one after one's death, land has ceased to be either a profit or a pleasure. It gives one position, and prevents one from keeping it up. That's all that can be said about land.

(4) ALGERNON: Well, I'm hungry.
JACK: I never knew you when you weren't . . .

(5) CHASUBLE: I hope, Cecily, you are not inattentive.
CECILY: Oh, I am afraid I am.
CHASUBLE: That is strange. Were I fortunate enough to be Miss Prism's pupil, I would hang upon her lips. [Miss Prism *glares*] I spoke metaphorically. – My metaphor was drawn from bees. Ahem!

(6) CECILY: I can't understand how you are here at all. Uncle Jack won't be back till Monday afternoon.
ALGERNON: That is a great disappointment. I am obliged to go up by the first train on Monday morning. I have a business appointment that I am anxious . . . to miss.
CECILY: Couldn't you miss it anywhere but in London?
ALGERNON: No: the appointment is in London.

(7) JACK: Oh! I don't see much fun in being christened along with other babies. It would be childish.

(8) ALGERNON: Darling! And when was the engagement actually settled?
CECILY: On the 14th of February last. Worn out by your entire ignorance of my existence, I determined to end the matter one way or the other, and after a long struggle with myself I accepted you under this dear old tree here. The next day I bought this little ring in your name, and this is the little bangle with the true lovers' knot I promised you always to wear.
ALGERNON: Did I give you this? It's very pretty, isn't it?
CECILY: Yes, you've wonderfully good taste, Ernest.

(9) CECILY: You must not laugh at me, darling, but it had always been a girlish dream of mine to love some one whose name was Ernest . . . There is something in that name that seems to inspire absolute confidence. I pity any poor married woman whose husband is not called Ernest.

(10) LADY BRACKNELL: May I ask if it is in this house that your invalid friend Mr Bunbury resides?
ALGERNON: (*Stammering*) Oh! No! Bunbury doesn't live here. Bunbury is somewhere else at present. In fact, Bunbury is dead.
LADY BRACKNELL: Dead! When did Mr Bunbury die?
ALGERNON: (*Airily*) Oh! I killed Bunbury this afternoon.

Sample answers

Quotation 1: In this quotation, Jack informs his friend Algernon that he in fact leads a double life. Jack explains that, as the guardian of Miss Cecily Cardew, he is forced in her presence to be completely moral at all times, and in all that he says, for he has to set her a good example. His moral behaviour and beliefs are a mask, though, and a rather stifling one. So, for the sake of his health and happiness, he has invented a wicked younger brother called Ernest, who lives in London and periodically gets into serious trouble. Using this fictitious brother as an excuse, Jack is able to visit London whenever he pleases. In

London, he leads a life of pleasure under the name of Ernest Worthing, and woos the beautiful Gwendolen Fairfax.

This quotation is central, for it reveals that Jack is leading a double life very similar to the one that Dorian Gray led in *The Picture of Dorian Gray*. Like Dorian, Jack behaves morally only when his social environment forces him to, but disappears for long periods during which he gives expression to his real self, which is wicked. His situation, however, reduces to harmlessness and innocence the perilous and evil double life of Dorian. Had Dorian been exposed in his lifetime, he would have been ruined and imprisoned. But Jack's exposure in *The Importance of Being Earnest* leads to no such thing. Quite the contrary, when Algy finds him out, their friendship deepens, for it turns out that Algy too leads a double life. The exposure of the pair later on leads paradoxically not to their social ruin but to marriage. Through Jack and Algy, Wilde in *The Importance of Being Earnest* reduces to playful innocence the dangerous situation of Dorian. In the paradise of childlike innocence that Wilde creates in *The Importance of Being Earnest*, evil is an unreal thing and it seems that no one can come to any harm.

A good example of this is Jack's 'killing' of his younger brother and Algy's 'murder' of Bunbury. In both 'Lord Arthur Savile's Crime' and *The Picture of Dorian Gray*, a murder is committed: Arthur kills Podgers and Dorian murders Basil Hallward. In *The Importance of Being Earnest*, the people who are 'murdered' are fictitious: they are figments of the imagination of Jack and Algy. In the play's world of childlike innocence, murder, like all acts of sin and evil, is unreal, a harmless and farcical thing.

Quotation 2: In this quotation, Jack tells Gwendolen that she is perfect, but she immediately rejects the idea, and for the rather nonsensical reason that perfection leaves no room for developments. In the fairy tale 'Lord Arthur Savile's Crime', Wilde had actually presented us with a perfect and pure girl, Sibyl, with whom Arthur was very much in love. Sibyl was presented as being both physically and spiritually perfect, and Arthur had to purge himself of all evil before he could marry her. Gwendolen is a parody of Sibyl. Physically beautiful, Gwendolen is nonetheless quite vain. She displays an ill temper in her encounter with Cecily. After she discovers that Jack is a liar who periodically goes up to London on pleasure trips, she quickly forgives him and agrees to marry him. Unlike Sibyl, Gwendolen is not spiritually perfect, nor does she require a pure husband. Quite the contrary, she finds the very idea of perfection rather amusing and nonsensical. When Algy makes a similar remark to Cecily in Act II, he is faced with a largely similar reaction that takes him aback. In *The*

Importance of Being Earnest, Sibyl is reduced to hilarious nonsense in the portrayal of Gwendolen and Cecily.

This quotation is a good example of how *The Importance of Being Earnest* functions, for in this play Wilde reduces to nonsense the major ideas and situations of his earlier works. His presentation of Jack and Algy, for instance, is a reduction to absurdity of the serious, dangerous, and sinful double life that Dorian Gray led in *The Picture of Dorian Gray*.

Quotation 3: The Importance of Being Earnest is a nonsense play, and in it Wilde renders absurd the various serious ideas he had expressed in his earlier works. In 'The Soul of Man Under Socialism', Wilde had argued in favour of the abolition of private property and stated rather wittily that this is in the interests of the rich, for the ownership of large stretches of land is a great bother. In *The Importance of Being Earnest*, Lady Bracknell, the main representative of the British aristocracy, is obviously a capitalist who is inflexible in her insistence that the class system should be preserved. In the quotation, however, she agrees fully with Wilde's earlier views concerning private property. The ownership of land to any large extent gives one position, she says, but gives neither profit nor pleasure. But her solution to the problem is a purely capitalistic one, which is to sell the land and invest the money. Lady Bracknell's position on the question of private property renders amusing and nonsensical Wilde's earlier views on socialism.

There is nonsense also in the dialogue of the quotation. Among the inconveniences of land, according to Lady Bracknell, are 'the duties exacted from one after one's death' – a totally absurd statement, since money is of no value to a dead person. *The Importance of Being Earnest* is a nonsense play not only because it reduces to absurdity the basic ideas and situations of Wilde's earlier works, but also because its dialogue is heavily nonsensical.

Another idea that is treated farcically in *The Importance of Being Earnest* is the concept of determinism. In 'Lord Arthur Savile's Crime', Arthur was presented as predestined by an external force. In *The Picture of Dorian Gray*, Dorian is predetermined by an inner force, his character and appetites. Wilde reduces this idea to mirthful nonsense in *The Importance of Being Earnest*, for when Algy proposes to Cecily, he discovers that he is already engaged to her. She then proceeds to give him a detailed history of their engagement. Algy's future being predetermined, it did not wait for him to bring it about, but occurred without him!

Essay questions

These are essay questions that may appear on an examination. Before you try to answer an essay question, you should write a brief outline of your main ideas. The outline will help you to clarify and to organise the basic points you wish to make. Using the outline as your guide, you should then proceed to write your essay. If you cannot produce a clear outline, this means that the answer is foggy in your mind and that you will not be able to write a good essay.

(1) In *The Importance of Being Earnest*, Oscar Wilde pairs characters and he also splits his characters into two contrasting groups. Explain how he does this, and why.

(2) Discuss Jack and Algy as a reduction to absurdity of the double life that Dorian Gray led.

(3) Discuss *The Importance of Being Earnest* as a play that seeks to create a mood of childlike innocence.

(4) Can *The Importance of Being Earnest* be described as a nonsense play? Discuss.

(5) *The Importance of Being Earnest* has sometimes been called a comedy of manners. Pass judgement on this categorisation of the play.

(6) Write a detailed character analysis of Cecily Cardew.

(7) What is Oscar Wilde's attitude towards predestination in *The Importance of Being Earnest*? Discuss this attitude in relation to two of Wilde's earlier works.

(8) Discuss Wilde's attitude towards socialism and the lower classes in the play.

(9) '*The Importance of Being Earnest* satirises Victorian society.' Argue for or against this point of view.

Sample answer

Question (1): In *The Importance of Being Earnest*, Oscar Wilde pairs characters and he also splits his characters into two contrasting groups. Explain how he does this, and why.

In *The Importance of Being Earnest*, Oscar Wilde's main purpose was to create a mood of innocence and nonsense. To do this, he did not need to present many characters who are elaborately drawn. Quite the contrary, the need was for simplicity, so he gave us relatively few characters and resorted to the rather simple device of pairing and contrasting them.

Jack and Algernon, for instance, are paired in the play. It is discovered in the end that they are actually brothers, but Wilde establishes them as brothers in spirit from the very beginning. Early in Act I, we learn that they both lead double lives. Jack leads a life of pleasure in London under the name of Ernest Worthing, while he wears the mask of Victorian morality in the country. Algy behaves morally in London, but he has invented an invalid friend whom he calls Bunbury and who lives in the country. This enables him to go to the country on a pleasure trip whenever he wishes. Moreover, Jack is in love with Gwendolen as the play opens, and Algy falls in love with Cecily in Act II. The girls insist on marrying a man with the name of Ernest, so Jack and Algy both seek to be rechristened under that name. Both men commit 'murder' in the play. Jack finds it convenient to 'kill' his fictitious brother Ernest, while Algernon 'murders' Bunbury. In many respects, then, Jack and Algy are exactly the same. Wilde meant them primarily as a reduction to harmless nonsense of the evil double life of Dorian Gray. The 'murders' they commit are an innocent and nonsensical version of Dorian's murder of the painter Basil Hallward and of Lord Arthur Savile's killing of Podgers.

Cecily and Gwendolen arc also paired in *The Importance of Being Earnest*. Although not sisters, they agree in Act II to call each other 'sister', and they are indeed sisters in personality. They both insist, quite nonsensically, that the man they marry should be called Ernest, thus causing Jack and Algy a lot of trouble. Gwendolen overwhelms Jack with her wit, and Cecily similarly overwhelms Algy. Both girls resist any attempt to attribute perfection to them. Their imperfection is revealed by their vanity and by the fact that they both accept wicked husbands in the end. In fact, Wilde presents them as a playful reduction to absurdity of the idea of a perfect and pure woman that is so prominent in 'Lord Arthur Savile's Crime'.

Dr Chasuble and Miss Prism are much alike. They are both guardians of the moral code. Miss Prism, for instance, is very severe in her condemnation of Jack's wicked younger brother Ernest. Dr Chasuble is quite interested in living according to the strict moral principles of the Primitive Church, especially as regards marriage. Both are very serious in their dealings with other people. Both, however – much like the prophet Jokanaan in *Salomé* – make slips of the tongue that reveal deep and repressed sexual longings. The marriage of these two characters at the end of the play underlines their similarity.

And yet Dr Chasuble and Miss Prism stand in contrast to Jack, Algernon, Gwendolen, and Cecily. The first group insists that all behaviour should be measured against a strict moral code, while the second is gay and pleasure-seeking.

The only character who does not seem to fit the pattern of pairing and contrasting is Lady Bracknell, but this is perhaps because she stands opposed to everybody else in the play. She has her own code of behaviour, which is that of the British aristocracy, and she spends the entire play trying unsuccessfully to force the other characters to behave according to it.

The main reason Wilde pairs and contrasts the characters of *The Importance of Being Earnest* is to achieve simplicity. His chief concern in the play is to create an atmosphere of innocence and nonsense through the dialogue and the behaviour of a few characters, and to reduce to absurdity the basic ideas and situations of his earlier works. The dialogue of *The Importance of Being Earnest* is of major significance. A large number of characters, presented in a complex manner, would have drawn attention away from the dialogue. Instead, Wilde wanted the focus to fall on the dialogue and on a few basic ideas and situations, such as the double lives that Jack and Algy lead, or their obsession with changing their names rather than undergoing a real spiritual rebirth. Thus, simplicity in characterisation was necessary.

Part 5
Suggestions for further reading

Wilde's works

The works that Wilde wrote before *The Importance of Being Earnest* are necessary reading for the serious student of this play. This is especially true of 'Lord Arthur Savile's Crime', *The Picture of Dorian Gray*, and *Salomé*. These are available on the market in several inexpensive editions.

A single volume containing *Lady Windermere's Fan, A Woman of No Importance, An Ideal Husband, The Importance of Being Earnest*, and *Salomé* is available in the Penguin Plays series, Penguin Books, Harmondsworth, 1954.

Biography

Richard Ellmann is currently preparing what will probably be the definitive biography of Wilde. In the meantime, the best biography remains Hesketh Pearson's *Oscar Wilde, His Life and Wit*, Methuen, London, 1946.

Criticism

Although Wilde has attracted many biographers, his writings have been strangely neglected by literary critics. The following critical material may prove useful:

BENTLEY, ERIC: *The Playwright as Thinker*, Reznal and Hitchcock, New York, 1946. This book contains an analysis of *The Importance of Being Earnest*. The argument is that the play's dialogue constitutes an anti-Victorian barrage, a sustained attack on everything the Victorians held sacred.

ELLMANN, RICHARD: 'Introduction: The Artist as Critic as Wilde.' In *The Artist as Critic: Critical Writings of Oscar Wilde*, edited by Richard Ellmann, Random House, New York, 1968. This article touches on *The Importance of Being Earnest* and argues that its main theme is sin and crime, but reduced to harmlessness.

NASSAAR, CHRISTOPHER S.: *Into the Demon Universe: A Literary Exploration of Oscar Wilde*, Yale University Press, New Haven and London, 1974. This is a book-length critical study of all of Wilde's major works. *The Importance of Being Earnest* is analysed in detail as a play in which Wilde tries to escape from evil by creating a world of innocence and nonsense. The argument is that Wilde reduces his previous works to the level of absurdity in *The Importance of Being Earnest*.

The author of these notes

CHRISTOPHER S. NASSAAR was educated at the American University of Beirut (BA), the University of Sussex (MA) and the University of Wisconsin (PHD). He has written on Rossetti and Wilde; his book *Into the Demon Universe: A Literary Exploration of Oscar Wilde* was published in 1974. He is at present an assistant Professor of English and Cultural Studies at the American University of Beirut.